The OUTCOME Primers Series 2.0
The CONTENT Primer

Other Books in This Series

The OUTCOME Primer:
Envisioning Learning Outcomes

The ASSESSMENT Primer:
Assessing and Tracking Evidence of Learning Outcomes

The MAPPING Primer:
Mapping the Way to Learning Outcomes

The GUIDING Primer:
Guiding Toward Learning Outcomes

The SUSTAINABILITY Primer:
Sustaining Learning Outcomes and Assessment

THE CONTENT PRIMER
ALIGNING ESSENTIAL CONTENT WITH LEARNING OUTCOMES

Ruth Stiehl
Founder, The Learning Organization
Professor Emeritus, Instructional Systems
Oregon State University

Michele Decker
Outcome Strategist, The Learning Organization
Professor of Nursing
Central Oregon Community College

The Learning Organization

The CONTENT Primer:
Aligning Essential Content with Learning Outcomes

Ruth Stiehl and Michele Decker

Print Edition Copyright © 2017
The Learning Organization
Corvallis, Oregon
Library of Congress Cataloging Number: 2016901248
ISBN: 978-1523496655

Executive Editor: Don Prickel
Assistant Editor: Lori Sours
Editor/Production: Robin McBride
Graphics and Illustrations: Geoffrey Floyd

CreateSpace Independent Publishing Platform, North Charleston, SC

For further information, visit our website at *www.outcomeprimers.com*
or email us at *strategists@outcomeprimers.com*.

To our families

—RS, MD

Table of Contents

PART FOUR: *Continuing Your Learning*

Tell me, and I will forget. Show me, and I may remember. Involve me, and I will understand.
—Confucius, 450 BC

The Purpose of This Book Stated as a Learning Outcome

Working through this book should help build your capacity to:

Work to identify, delimit and align essential content with learning outcomes by designing backwards, outside in; design programs, courses and workshops from a contemporary, constructivist understanding of learning.

The OUTCOME Primers Series 2.0

The OUTCOME Primer: *Envisioning Learning Outcomes*

What do learners need to be able to do in real-life roles that we are responsible for in programs, courses, and workshops?

The ASSESSMENT Primer: *Assessing and Tracking Evidence of Learning Outcomes*

What can learners do to show evidence of the intended outcomes and how will the evidence be documented, tracked, and used?

The CONTENT Primer: *Aligning Essential Content with Learning Outcomes*

What concepts, skills, and issues are essential for learners to achieve the intended outcomes?

The MAPPING Primer: *Mapping the Way to Learning Outcomes*

How do we assure that the learner's journey aligns with the intended outcomes?

The GUIDING Primer: *Guiding Toward Learning Outcomes*

What do effective *guides* do that is so different from our traditional notion of *teaching*?

The SUSTAINABILITY Primer: *Sustaining Learning Outcomes and Assessment*

How do we create a system of learning outcomes and assessment so the work is sustained?

Once a Fad—Now a Fact!

When we published the very first OUTCOMES Primer in the year 2000, academic and workplace training programs were deemed a success based on seat time, bodies in the seats, and the number of topics covered; the transfer of learning to real-life roles was little more than an afterthought.

It has taken the past fifteen years for professional organizations and accreditation agencies to move the adult education industry into adopting an outcome-based framework for curricular planning.

The six Essential Questions addressed in
The OUTCOME Primers Series 2.0

- *What do learners need to be able to do in real-life roles that we are responsible for in programs, courses, and workshops?*

- *What can learners do to show evidence of the intended outcomes and how will the evidence be documented, tracked, and used?*

- *What concepts, skills, and issues are essential for the learners to achieve the intended outcomes?*

- *How do we assure that the learner's journey aligns with the intended outcomes?*

- *What do effective* guides *do that is so different from our traditional notion of "teaching"?*

- *How do we create a system of learning outcomes and assessments so the work is sustained?*

Once a fad, now a fact, implementing curricula that are driven by clear and robust learning outcomes is a major challenge for all education programs in universities, community, and technical colleges, as well as the workplace.

It is one thing for an organization to *own* the idea of learning outcomes, and quite another for it to create a sustainable system that includes six key actions: envisioning learning outcomes, aligning essential content with learning outcomes, assessing and tracking evidence of outcomes, mapping learning experiences, guiding learners toward the outcomes, and sustaining the process during other kinds of organizational change. Our newly released *OUTCOME Primers Series 2.0* is designed and structured to make every leader, instructor, and trainer proficient in these six areas of outcomes planning and assessment.

Distinguishing Our Work

If there were two primary things that distinguish our work with outcomes and assessment from all others, it would have to be the understanding of *outside-in* and *the learner's journey.*

In all six Primers, we have sought to apply systems thinking through the concept of *outside-in*—the simple notion that every learning experience is for a purpose outside the learning environment, meaning, in real-life contexts. Planning for a learning experience begins *outside.*

The second thing that distinguishes our work in the Primers is the concept of *the learner's journey.* If there is any unifying visual organizer that can clarify outcome-based learning and assessment in academic and workplace organizations, it is a paddler on a rapidly flowing whitewater river. To us, there is nothing more foundational to outcomes thinking than to carry a mental image of learners on their journey in an ever-changing river of life experiences. In *The GUIDING Primer: Guiding Toward Learning Outcomes,* we reinforce this image by picturing a paddle raft of learners on a whitewater river with the guide at the back, where every rapid is an opportunity to assess learning.

When we envision a workshop, training, course, or program as a sequence of learning experiences that flow from the first class session, *the put-in,* to the last class session, *the take-out,* there seems to be greater clarity about what it means to teach, train, or GUIDE (our preferred word) toward significant outcomes. It is this image of the *learner's journey* and *outside-in* that we carry throughout all the six Primers in this series, and capture, in its simplest form, on the following pages. These two primary distinguishing characteristics of the Primers are illustrated in the overleaf on pages xiv and xv.

While our approach to understanding outcomes and assessment has not changed from our first primer in 2000, it is quite a departure for us to break outcomes planning into six distinct Primers (a *six-pac*). There are three specific reasons we have selected this small format for our new Series:

- Each Primer highlights one important element in outcome-based planning and can be used independently for intensive professional development.
- We can produce quantities of individual primers inexpensively, meaning organizations can afford to get them in the hands of every trainer and every instructor, not just the leaders.
- Each Primer or the entire series of six books (a *six-pac*) can be printed and shipped literally overnight.

As always, there are trade-offs in keeping the purchase price low and separating the tasks. We have chosen to forego our desire to use color, high-end paper, and fold-out pages. We also take a risk in separating each element of outcomes and assessment from the *whole*; all systems are greater than the individual parts taken separately. The answer is to invest in the *whole*.

It is our hope that these books will prove as useful as the original series we began more than 15 years ago.

—Ruth Stiehl
Corvallis, Oregon
2017

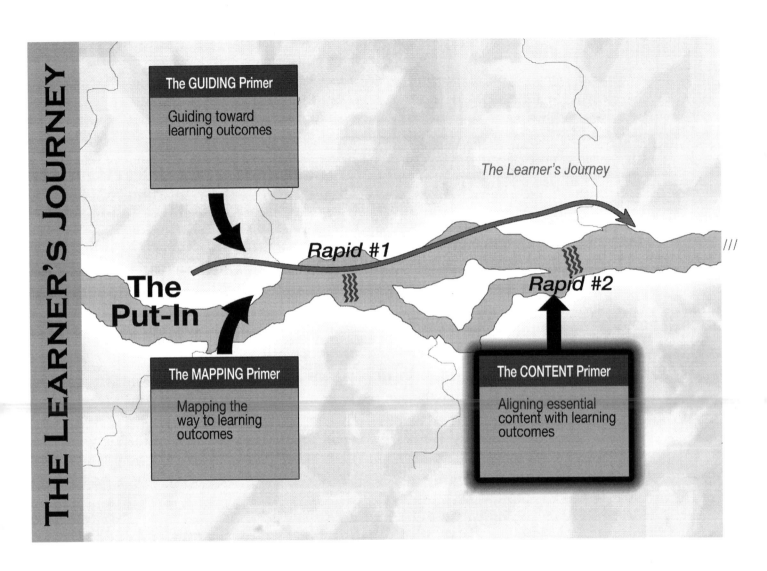

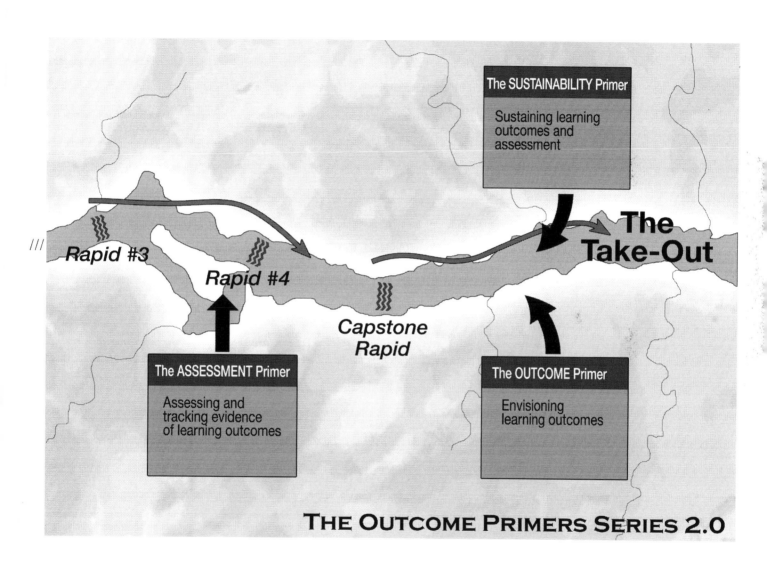

PART ONE
The Importance of Analyzing Outcomes First

Analyzing the intended learning outcomes to determine the essential content is one of the important marks of a strong curriculum.

Introduction

One of the greatest challenges in describing an outcome-based model for program, course, and workshop design in the college and workplace comes from the fact that it is not a linear process. Oh, how easy it would be if it were 1, 2, 3, 4, 5, 6. DONE! And yet, it's not entirely a non-linear process either. There is one thing that has to come first, and that is the intended learning outcome. Every other step in the process is quite fluid, so we like to say the process is *linear-ish*.

Linear-ish means that trying to pour outcome-based learning into six distinct books is like trying to pour a gallon bucket of spring water into six tiny bottles lined up in a row, each capturing a distinct part of that gallon. The fact is, the water spills all over the place. Likewise, you will find plenty of that *spilling* throughout the pages of all six primer books of *The OUTCOME Primers Series 2.0*. We think that's good, because it accurately reflects how the planning process, in reality, works.

The part we try to capture in *The CONTENT Primer* (that *spills* into other primers) is how to make decisions about what essential content (subject matter) an educational program, course, workshop, or training should include using an outcome design model. But these decisions can only be made once the first bottle is full, meaning, the intended outcomes are really clear enough to drive the decisions regarding what essential content must be understood by learners. Having a clear vision of where we want to go not only makes sense in planning for learning, it just might hold true in much of life itself.

Designing Backwards—Outside In

Outcome statements describe what learners should be able to do *outside* a classroom—not *inside* it!

In stating intended learning outcomes, we describe our hope for what learners will be able to do in real-life roles for which we have a responsibility. Defining and assessing learning outcomes are the most important tasks a training program or educational organization is asked to do.

When we first started our work over a decade ago, we used those swirling images as depicted in Figure 1 on the following page to visually define what we meant by the term *learning outcomes*. It implied that when we engage our energy in structured learning activities, results are likely to *spin off* from the clockwise action. So it follows that building an outcome-based curriculum reverses the flow; the flow is counter-clockwise, **outside-in.** We begin by envisioning results and then build the curriculum **backwards** that will best help our students realize the intended outcomes.

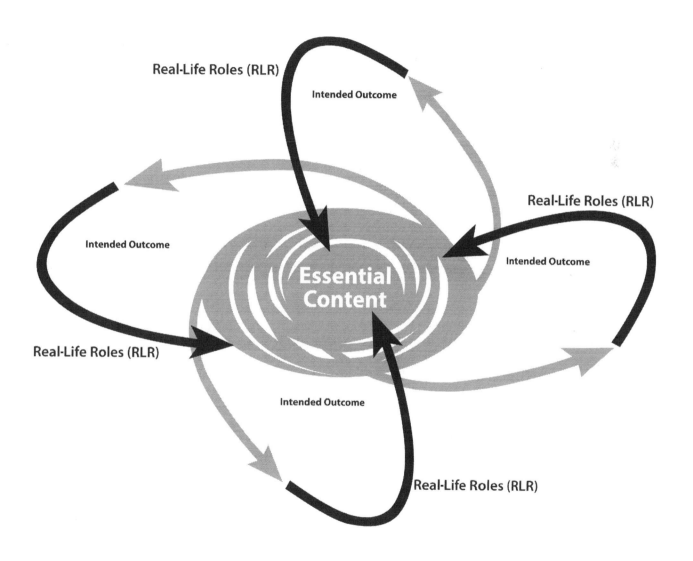

Figure 1: Designing Backwards, Outside-In

In today's educational climate, our constituents are asking us one primary question, "What can we expect learners to be able to do, in real-life roles, as a result of having completed specific learning experiences?" They want to know that the curriculum focuses on what learners need in order to succeed in the workplace, the family and the community, in the rest of life. Making these connections is something we may have done well in the past but find increasingly difficult in a rapidly changing society.

Since this Primer is part of a series that entails a whole systemic process, we are making the assumption at the beginning of this Primer that you are working from a set of statements that clearly describe the intended learning outcomes for a program, course, workshop or training. Because the quality of your outcome statements is so important to the rest of the planning, we encourage you to assess your outcome statements against the criteria in Figure 2: Scoring Guide—Assessing the Quality of Intended Outcome Statements on the following page.

If you feel your outcome statements may fall short of these standards, we recommend that you take a look at *The OUTCOME Primer: Envisioning Learning Outcomes* in preparation for doing the work described in this Primer.

Template: Scoring Guide—Assessing the Quality of Intended Outcome Statements					
Rating scale: 1=absent 2=minimally met 3=adequately met 4=exceptionally met					
Characteristics of Good Learning Outcome Statements					Suggestions/Improvements
1. Action	1	2	3	4	
All the statements are written in active voice, and the action words have been carefully chosen to describe the intention.					
2. Context	1	2	3	4	
All the statements describe what you envision students doing "after" and "outside" this academic experience—because of this experience.					
3. Scope	1	2	3	4	
Given the time and resources available, the outcome statements represent reasonable expectations for students.					
4. Complexity	1	2	3	4	
The statements, as a whole, have sufficient substance to drive decisions about what students need to learn in this experience.					
5. Brevity and Clarity	1	2	3	4	
The language is concise and clear, easily understood by students and stakeholders.					

Figure 2: Scoring Guide—Assessing the Quality of Intended Outcome Statements

PART TWO

Learning from the Past, Moving into the Future

The future belongs to a very different kind of person with a very different kind of mind—creators and empathizers, pattern recognizers, and meaning makers.

—Daniel Pink

A Paradigm Shift: The Place of Conceptual Learning in an Outcome-Based Model

Daniel Pink, author of several books that focus on the "changing workplace," suggests that we envision the last 150 years as progressing from the agriculture age (farmers), to the industrial age (factory workers), onto the information age (knowledge workers), and now to the 21st century, the conceptual age (creators and empathizers). While Pink provides us with a more academic description conceptually, Robert Lutz, top executive from General Motors, emphasizes that the current 21st century will require workers to possess *high-concept* and *high-touch* aptitudes. In other words, solving increasingly complex problems will require a knowledge of essential concepts (conceptual thinking) that can be applied to real-life work roles and societal situations.

Erickson (2007) characterizes conceptual thinking as "the ability to critically examine factual information, relate (factual information) to prior knowledge, see patterns and connections, draw out significant understanding at the conceptual level, evaluate the truth of the understanding based on the supporting evidence, transfer understanding across time or situation, and create a new product, process or idea."

Therefore, the premise of a conceptual theory of learning in an outcome-based model is that learners benefit from a deep understanding of core, essential concepts which serve as the framework to which they attach new knowledge. A concept approach helps instructors both manage excessive content and assist learners in transferring learning to new situations. This, of course, must be followed by creating an active learning environment with real-world learning activities that align with the intended learning outcomes.

One of the major concerns regarding outcome-based curriculum design models is that subject-focused content is somewhat lost. Actually, it is not lost at all, but it no longer comes first. Curriculum design isn't just a process of deciding what content is to be covered. It's a process of deciding what content learners must understand and master in order to achieve the intend outcomes. The outcomes justify the content. They give it purpose beyond learning content for the sake of content.

In the traditional classroom, content is presented as topics to be covered. In this new outcome-based framework, the focus is on understanding essential content necessary to achieve the intended learning outcomes. What learners need to understand is expressed conceptually in three ways: *concepts, skills, and issues*, all three of which will be explained in great detail in Part Three of this Primer.

Making the shift from *covering content* to *growing content* has enormous meaning for how learning activities will be designed. The educator becomes a facilitator and coach, and rather than asking, "What do I want to teach?", the educator asks, "What do students need to learn?" We know, for example, that the best way to introduce new content to learners is through the use of active learning strategies, real-world case scenarios and problems to be solved. For an in-depth view into active learning strategies, we refer you to *The GUIDING Primer: Guiding Toward Learning Outcomes.*

In professional-based studies and training, the creation of the curriculum has always been guided by the professional knowledge of instructors, subject matter experts, literature reviews, performance data, advisory boards, and job/role analysis. Now, more than ever, these many influences are calling for learning experiences that focus on outcome-based conceptual learning. Nursing studies is a good example.

A Case in Point: Nursing Studies

In 2006, Wake Technical Community College in North Carolina was awarded a two-year grant called the *Curriculum Improvement Project* consisting in the collaborative restructuring and revision of the Associate Degree Nursing Education Curricula of 55 nursing programs. Under the guidance of Dr. Jean Giddens, the nursing instructors from across the state set out to develop a curriculum based on a taxonomy of nursing concepts, as noted in Figure 3 on the following page.

Nursing programs across the country are beginning to adopt North Carolina's model, including my (Michele) program at Central Oregon Community College. But a word of caution is needed here. Often, the danger is that such a taxonomy may often be improperly presented as topics to be covered. In this new outcome-based framework, the focus is on understanding essential content necessary to achieve the intended learning outcomes. As I am writing this, we are reviewing all of our course and program level intended learning outcomes (done annually) and will soon begin another re-alignment of essential content necessary to achieve the intended learning outcomes.

Topics vs. Outcomes

In pre-21st century, a topic-focused model of instructional design drove everything: lecturing on topics, reading from textbooks, memorizing, reciting, testing over topics, and passing tests based on retention of topics. Instructors were hired solely for their knowledge of subject matter with little regard for skills as an educator to create life-focused outcomes. Lecturing was considered the best way to transfer knowledge to learners, as it was often considered the primary teaching strategy.

Under this topic-focused model, subject matter for courses was largely derived from and sequenced by textbook chapters whether it was important or not to the

Biophysical Concepts	Psychosocial Concepts	Reproductive Concepts	Nursing Domain Concepts	Healthcare Domain Concepts
Acid-Base Balance	Addiction	Antepartum Care	Assessment	Accountability
Cellular Regulation	Cognition	Intrapartum Care	Caring Interventions	Advocacy
Comfort	Culture and Diversity	Postpartum Care	Clinical Decision Making	Ethics
Digestion	Developmental	Newborn Care	Collaboration	Evidence-based Practice
Elimination	Family	Prematurity	Communication	Healthcare Systems
Fluids and Electrolytes	Grief and Loss		Managing Care	Health Policy
Health-Wellness-Illness	Mood and Affect		Professional Behaviors	Informatics
Immunity	Self		Teaching and Learning	Legal Issues
Infection	Spirituality			Quality Improvement
Inflammation	Stress and Coping			Safety
Intracranial Regulation	Violence			
Metabolism				
Mobility				
Nutrition				
Oxygenation				
Perfusion				
Perioperative Care				
Sensory Perception				
Sexuality				
Thermoregulation				
Tissue Integrity				

Source: *adn-cip.waketech.edu/concept_curriculum.html*

Figure 3: North Carolina Nursing Curriculum Improvement Project

learner. Topics for workplace training were supplied by the technical expert who knew the most and often provided far more information than what was needed to do a job. An instructor's sense of success was whether or not s/he got through all the material. It is important to understand topic-focused thinking because many of our practices in education and training still reflect this *old school* model.

Back in 2006, I (Ruth) took the opportunity at a national conference to ask 90 college presidents and vice presidents the following question in a face-to-face meeting: "What is the very first thing you should do in planning to teach a course*?*"

Here are the two most common responses:

"Take the topics from a previous syllabus", and

"Find out what textbook others are using".

Answers similar to these made up 82% of the responses from college leaders in the room.

Take a closer look. What do these responses have in common? There are two things both statements say: 1) Knowing what to *cover* is the place to begin planning a course, and 2) Learning is about what the *instructor does*, not what the *student will do*.

While the answers did not surprise me, it seemed to surprise those in the room. I understood that it was just the way we had been thinking in higher education for a very long time. I can only guess that the response from the workplace training director may have been similar. Perhaps it would have been:

"List the KSA's."

So, what are KSAs about? In the mid-20th century, there was a movement based on a behavioral theory of learning that germinated widely. The content for training programs was expressed as *knowledge, skills and attitudes* (KSA's) and saw wide acceptance in workplace training and parts of higher education. The negative effect of the movement was the reduction of learning to the lowest level of cognitive tasks.

The one positive contribution of the behavioral movement that still exists today in outcome-based learning is the focus on what the learner does, rather than on what the instructor does. Instead of the instructor covering topics, students were learning knowledge, skills and attitudes, *and that is a major shift in thinking and planning!* This change began to focus our attention on learning even though the reductionist nature of the movement led to disconnected, shallow learning.

In a 21st century outcome-based model for learning, the appropriate answer to the question of what comes first in curriculum planning should be:

> "Describe the intended learning outcomes."

One of the reasons outcome-based learning is so widely embraced throughout education today is that it retains what worked from the behavioral theories, but greatly deepens learning with an emphasis on constructing meaning that reflects a new understanding of how the living brain actually learns. To fully understand outcome-based learning we will need to shift our understanding of learning itself.

For example, current neurological research tells us that when we learn something new, the brain literally establishes new branches between cells called dendrites. Repeated exposure and interaction with new content causes dendrites to form thicker branches, allowing signals (thinking) to travel faster and with less interference. Synapses develop between dendrites to promote memory. It is the continued growth of this complex network that we describe as *deeper learning*.

For deeper learning to occur, therefore, we align only that which is essential content in the form of *concepts, skills, and issues* with the intended learning outcomes. In Part Three, you will learn to distinguish those essential *concepts, skills, and issues* necessary for deeper learning. This deep under-standing of such essential content provides the foundation necessary for learners to demonstrate proficiency in the intended learning outcomes of programs, courses, workshops, and trainings.

PART THREE
Distinguishing Concepts, Issues, and Skills

"An inch deep and a mile wide."

—Schmidt, McKnight and Raizen

The Consequences of Information Overload

In our technological world of ever expanding information, the amount of content found in programs, courses, workshops, and trainings can be so massive that learners fail to achieve a deep understanding of anything, resulting in the lack of transfer of learning to real-life application. It is a prevalent problem at every level of training and education. Instructors and learners alike are often exhausted, frustrated victims of the assumption that we have to *know it all*. We refer to this kind of learning as "an inch deep and a mile wide".

One contributor to this shared feeling of frustration over trying to *know it all* is the extraordinarily rapid pace at which information is increasing. As knowledge increases, so too does the pressure to include all encompassing levels of subject matter content into a constrained learning time frame. We refer to this as an *additive curriculum*. As a health science educator, I (Michele) frequently feel personally responsible for covering *all* of the content with students whether or not it is essential to the intended outcome. Often the result is a form of shallow learning that does not transfer to other learning or real-life applications.

A second contributor to information overload (and shallow learning) is the ease of access to information through new technologies. What used to be difficult to find is now right at our fingertips.

Too often the result of easy access to increased knowledge means cramming more and more content into programs, courses, and workshops, while removing nothing. The result is reducing learning to a superficial level. A bloated curriculum fails to support deep understanding of concepts, critical thinking of issues, and application of skills to real-life situations. These are the attributes that are so highly valued in a quality education.

For example, I (Michele) teach a class on acute kidney injury—where a person's kidneys abruptly lose the ability to create urine. For the learner to understand why this happens and how the person's well-being will be affected, we look at the underlying disease process.

Before entering my class, all of our students have completed four terms of sophomore-level anatomy and physiology, and three terms in the Nursing program of studies. When we begin to discuss the disruption of the regulatory systems of the kidney, the classroom goes quiet, eyes focus to their table tops, and sometimes whimpering can be heard! "How many of you recall the renin-angiotensin-aldosterone regulatory system?" my voice echoes around the room. The faculty calls this *previously learned knowledge*, and without the transfer of this essential knowledge, learning halts. There is nothing to build upon. If there is a lack of understanding of this regulatory system, it is impossible for the learner to think critically about the holistic effects and potential complications a person would experience.

Such understanding is essential, and if not mastered, learning of this regulatory system must be reviewed or relearned.

Without deep knowledge of essential content, our nursing graduates would be reduced to providing superficial task-oriented care of patients. I don't know about you, but I want a nurse who can think critically about my health situation and provide me with care based on a deep understanding of their discipline and a proficiency in skills to address my health issues.

In short, two principles ring out in order to avoid information overload. *Less content is better than more*. We call this *lean* learning and it is one way to better manage the vast amount of information we think we have to teach and learners have to understand. In addition, to reduce the amount of content overload, an analysis must be conducted to differentiate between all the content and the essential content. Thus, *choose only content that is essential to achieving the intended learning outcome.* Understanding and applying these two principles can greatly reduce the pressure that teachers often carry in feeling obliged to *cover everything* and for learners to *know it all*.

So, what are some of the specific ways we can resist information overload in our programs, courses, workshops and trainings in the interest of deeper learning? Here are four things you can do now:

1. Let go of the perceived personal responsibility to *cover everything. (This is a tough one for academics.)*
2. Collaborate with constituents to develop learning outcomes that are relevant to real-life roles.
3. Collaborate with constituents to identify and prioritize only content that is essential to achieving the desired learning outcomes.
4. Be reasonable about how much can be learned in a given period of time.

Expressing Content as Concepts, Issues, and Skills

Out of habit, and even when we have a set of learning outcomes, when we begin to think about what content should be included in a given program, course or workshop, it is tempting to continue expressing content as *topics.* When we do this, we aren't yet thinking in terms of deeper learning. To help break this habit, throughout this book we define essential content threefold: *concepts, issues and skills.*

The use of *concepts, issues and skills* in curriculum planning places the focus squarely on essential content and helps us limit information overload. In preparation for the remainder of this Primer, we provide here simple definitions along with several examples of how *concepts, issues, and skills* might be expressed in a program, course, or workshop. We will expand on these definitions and examples throughout the rest of this Primer.

Take a look at Figure 4 on the following page. Note carefully the arrows indicating how the *concepts, issues and skills* all originate from an analysis of the intended outcome, again *designing backwards, outside in*.

<u>Note:</u> Attempting to put content into three *circle clusters* (as we have done here) is convenient for planning, but it doesn't really tell the truth. The truth is, boundaries blur. *Concepts, issues and skills* are interwoven in highly complex ways none of us fully understands.

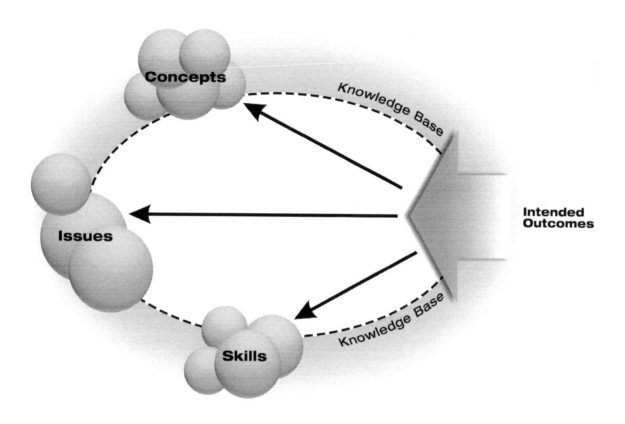

Figure 4: Analyzing Outcomes to Determine Content

Outcome-based curriculum designers work carefully to discover the essential macro and micro *concepts, issues and skills* that are critical to achieving the intended outcomes. At every turn in building the essential content, the designer focuses on three standing questions:

> ***QUESTION 1:*** What **concepts** do learners need to *understand* in order to demonstrate the intended learning outcomes?

Concepts make up our major mental framework. Concepts identify what learners must come to understand. It is this mental understanding to which we attach new learning and enables us to elevate our thinking to a level of abstraction. Conceptual learning promotes deep learning that is more important than collecting and attempting to recall disconnected information.

We can think of concepts as the major ideas that learners need to understand to achieve the intended outcomes. Concepts are typically represented by a list of words that have universal application and appear timeless. Each important concept can usually be expressed in as little as 1 to 3 words.

Examples of **concepts**:

- assembly language, macros, micros, processors (from a computer programming course)
- grammaticality, main idea, modifiers, organization (from a writing course)
- bone loss, bone density, estrogen, fractures (from a workshop on preventing osteoporosis)

QUESTION 2: What **issues** must learners be able to *resolve* in order to demonstrate the intended learning outcomes?

QUESTION 3: What **skills** must learners *develop* in order to demonstrate the intended learning outcomes?

Issues is a word we use to express the need for critical thinking—a deeper form of learning. Issues identify challenges learners must be able to resolve. Learning outcomes that relate to real-life roles are laden with problems and dilemmas that demand a deep level of critical thinking and decision-making. Making issues a major part of a learning plan assures that critical thinking is embedded in the learning experience.

Skills are most easily defined by how learners develop them; learners develop skills through a routine of practice and feedback. Skills identify what learners must be able to do if they are to show evidence that they have attained the intended outcome. There are both psycho-motor and cognitive skills. In both, learning happens through modeling, repetitive practice and appropriate feedback, all focused on a performance standard.

*Examples of **issues**:*

- remedy viruses, debug message errors (from a computer programming course)
- writer's block, fear of criticism (from a writing course)
- unaware of risk factors, disregard for exercise (from a workshop on osteoporosis)

*Examples of **skills**:*

- use algorithms, flowchart a program, conduct debugging procedures (from a computer programming course)
- construct cohesive paragraphs, fix grammatical errors, write clear main idea sentences (from a writing course)

—assess own risk factors, plan an exercise and nutrition treatment routine, keep current with literature (from workshop on preventing osteoporosis)

Posting Content onto the Outcome Guide: Pogging Cogging, and Wogging

You have just learned that the essential content of a course, program or workshop is expressed as *concepts, issues and skills.* We have also developed a curriculum template, introduced in *The OUTCOME Primer: Envisioning Learning Outcomes,* that can be used to display this essential content in any program, course, workshop or training.

If you have not read *The OUTCOME Primer: Envisioning Learning Outcomes,* here is the good news. The basic plan for most outcome-based programs, courses, and workshops can be placed on just one page or screen. Really! Just one page! The challenge is

that a great deal of thought must go in to the words that end up on that page.

This single page template, referred to as an Outcome Guide and shown in Figure 5, on the following page, can be used interchangeably, whether you are designing a program, course, workshop or training, as shown by the abbreviations (POG for program, COG for a course, WOG for a workshop or training). We use these abbreviations to describe the level at which you are designing. If you are designing a course, you are *Cogging,* a workshop or training, *Wogging,* or a program of studies, *Pogging.* Confusing? We describe this process in great detail at the end of this section, *Determining Essential Content: A Facilitator's Guide,* pages 49–60. (You will find this and other templates in digital form on our web site, *www.outcomeprimers.com.* Permission is granted to copy any of the templates in *The OUTCOME Primers Series 2.0 as long as the source is cited.)*

COG TITLE: _____   Date: _____

Concepts & Issues	Skills	Assessment Tasks	Intended Outcomes
What must the learners understand to demonstrate the intended outcome?	What skills must the learners master to demonstrate the intended outcome?	What will learners do in here to demonstrate evidence of the outcome?	What do learners need to be able to DO "out there" in the rest of life that we're responsible for "in here"?

What issues must the learners be able to resolve to demonstrate the outcome?

Figure 5: Template—Course Outcome Guide (COG)

Your task here, in using the Template—Outcome Guide, will be to begin inserting the essential *concepts, issues and skills* into their respective columns. *The OUTCOME Primer: Envisioning Learning Outcomes* provides the process for first creating clear and robust learning outcomes. Before doing so, first take a look at an example.

Figure 6 shows a completed Course Outcome Guide for one of the many courses required for the masters degree program in adult education at Oregon State University. The course, *Adult Education 531 (AED 531): Instructional Design,* was *designed backwards, by first analyzing the outcomes* (right to left), to determine the essential content, i.e., the key *concepts, issues and skills* for AED 531. Notice the column to the left of the outcome statements identifies the *performance tasks/assessments* asked of learners in order to demonstrate proficiency of the learning outcomes. These are not addressed in this Primer, but described in detail in *The ASSESSMENT Primer: Assessing and Tracking Evidence of Learning Outcomes.*

Remember the process is only linear-ish; thinking through assessment can come before or after thinking about essential content, whichever works best in a given subject area. The linear thing to remember is that outcomes always come FIRST!

POG/COG/WOG TITLE: COG: AED531—Instructional Design   **Date:** _____

Concepts & Issues	Skills	Assessment Tasks	Intended Outcomes
What must the learners understand to demonstrate the intended outcome?	*What skills must the learners master to demonstrate the intended outcome?*	*What will learners do in here to demonstrate evidence of the outcome?*	*What do learners need to be able to DO "out there" in the rest of life that we're responsible for "in here"?*
-Curriculum frameworks -Envisioning learning -Systematic/systemic -Open/closed systems -Analysis/synthesis -Both/and -Systems thinking -Zoom -Boundaries; layers -Self-organizing -Feedback loops -Disturbance/change -Learning outcomes -Process skills -Performance tasks	Program Level: --Identify an instructional need --Use interview, affinity group or focus group techniques --State program outcomes clearly in performance terms --Design-down concepts and process skills from outcomes (POG) --Identify performance tasks --Create program maps Course Level: --Design-down the essential concepts and process skills for courses in the program --Create a course COG --Prepare a course syllabus/training guide --Prepare scoring guides Lesson/Activity Level: --Plan learning activities for specific concepts or process skills that integrate the seven factors of learner success	Level 1: Program Level Design-down an outcome-based instructional program (college or workplace) that includes: -Tool 1: Outcome Detail -Tool 2: Program Map -Tool 3: Program Outcome Guide (POG) Level 2: Course Level Design-down an outcome-based college course or training module that consists of Tool 2: Course Outcome Guide & Syllabus Level 3: Instructional Level Design an outcome-based learning experience (college or workplace) that addresses the factors of learner success	1. Use systemic and strategic thinking to design college curriculum and teaching in the context of the 21st Century (the Age of Paradox). 2. Use systemic and strategic thinking to create effective learning experiences in the high performance work place of the 21st Century.

• Learner-centered facilitation
• Criteria/scoring guides

What issues must the learners be able to resolve to demonstrate the outcome?

Figure 6: AED 531—Instructional Design

What Concepts Must Your Learners Understand?

Concepts are major ideas learners must understand. Throughout *The OUTCOME Primers Series 2.0*, we use a variety of organic systems (like a river) to help us better visualize and understand the factors that are essential to an outcome-based curriculum design. Here is a visual image that might help clarify and distinguish how concepts function in any given program, course, workshop or workplace training event.

It was early spring when I (Ruth) recognized that I needed to do some serious repair on my back lawn before the rains ended (no hurry—that could be July in Oregon). I had taken out a large bush from the middle of the lawn the previous fall and seeded the area with grass, but over the winter the grass had died.

Oregon grows about 80% of the world's grass seed. So on my *do it yourself* trip to the garden store, there was a wide assortment of seed to choose from, including 'Speedy Green' - the same seed I had chosen the previous fall. But on this visit I noticed a large sign over the grass seed section which read, "Caution: Speedy Green will not winter over. It's meant for a quick fix only."

I had planted a grass seed mixture that was 93.5% annual ryegrass and only 5.8% perennial. It was all laid out in the small print: "Fast starting, fills in quickly and gets you through one season." I had made a big mistake, but so had others. Therefore the caution, I suppose. Ever the teacher, I went home wondering how much *Speedy Green* I had planted in the minds of learners over the years, knowledge that didn't *winter over*.

So I began looking for another metaphor, one that would paint a picture of conceptual learning. I found it in an orchard.

In Oregon, we have many kinds of orchards that do well in the rain: hazelnuts, apples, pears, peaches and cherries galore. They often grow side-by-side with the grass seed fields. Contrast a blade of grass with a hazelnut tree. Then think of each hazelnut tree as a concept, each beginning as a slight twig of meaning and, over time, growing into a complex network of branches that form a broad canopy of understanding. Old hazelnut orchards become so integrated that even the boundaries between individual trees are eventually blurred. Sound familiar? This is the same picture we painted earlier of how the brain naturally learns, emerging, connecting and integrating over time. It's very different from planting annual ryegrass that totally disappears after a season.

When we work with instructors to develop an Outcome Guide, we always get the question, "How many concepts should I list for a course, or for a program: 8,12,15?" We have learned to answer their question with another question, "How many hazelnut trees can you grow in a half-acre?" In the interest of deeper learning, the answer is, "as many as you have space for (time for) and no more."

A program, course or workshop guide (POG, COG, WOG) ideally includes up to ten (10) carefully identified words or phrases that describe the essential concepts about which the learners must discover some depth of meaning in order to achieve the learning outcomes. More detailed plans may include further sub-concepts.

Figure 7, on the following page, shows the essential concepts required in the teaching of the course, WR20–30, Fundamentals of Composition. First study carefully the identified concepts and examine how they align with the learning outcome statements.

POG/COG/WOG TITLE: _COG: WR20-30—Fundamentals of Composition_ _____ **Date:** _____

Concepts & Issues

What must the learners understand to demonstrate the intended outcome?

- Grammaticality
- Main idea
- Supporting detail
- Organization
- Spelling (sound/spelling correspondences)
- Clarity in writing
- Variety in writing
- The need for writing in further education and the workplace

---

- Writer's block
- Fears of criticism
- Chaos in life
- Time
- Inability to organize
- Being overwhelmed
- Not understanding the college culture

What issues must the learners be able to resolve to demonstrate the outcome?

Skills

What skills must the learners master to demonstrate the intended outcome?

- Generate ideas for a paper
- Write clear main idea statements
- Provide support for ideas
- Organize support coherently
- Construct paragraphs and essays
- Identify and fix ungrammatical, punctuation, and spelling errors
- Think critically about one's own work
- Organize one's work

Assessment Tasks

What will learners do in here to demonstrate evidence of the outcome?

1. Write a clear paragraph out of class, with few grammatical errors.
2. Write a clear multi-paragraph essay out of class, with few grammatical errors.
3. Write a coherent essay on a given topic in an "on demand" situation.

Intended Outcomes

What do learners need to be able to DO "out there" in the rest of life that we're responsible for "in here"?

1. Communicate written thought in a clear and organized manner to effectively inform, persuade, describe, and convey ideas in academic, work, community, and family settings.
2. Gather, evaluate, and present own "body of work."
3. Take responsibility for own learning by: managing own time, managing materials, following directions, communicating effectively, persistently pursuing own goals.

Figure 7: Essential Concepts in WR20–30, Fundamentals of Composition

What Issues Must Your Learners Resolve?

Issues provide learners with insight into outcome-related problems or concerns that will be faced in real-life roles. In the minds of many people, critical thinking is the single most important distinguishing characteristic of an educated person. We all think it sounds good, but making space for it in the curriculum is a different challenge. By making *issues* one of the three basic building blocks of essential content, we give critical thinking a new priority in all educational experiences, as it should be in an increasingly complex society.

When we express content as *issues*, we move to the essence of critical thinking: **analysis** *(taking issues apart),* **synthesis** *(putting ideas together),* **evaluation** *(making judgments about issues) and* **reflection** *(self-assessment of thinking, understanding, and problem-solving).* Identifying *issues* in a program, course or workshop encour-

ages an instructor to think about how critical thinking contributes to the outcome of every learning experience. In fact, the prominence of *issues* included on *outcome guides* across the curriculum is our best indication that critical thinking is valued and taught.

What distinguishes *issues* from *concepts* in an *outcome guide*? It is the need to resolve a problem or dilemma. When we envision outcomes in the context of real-life roles, there are always dilemmas and problems that are not present in a classroom. In this way, an outcome-based curriculum will always require a study of *issues* that require a level of problem-solving and critical thinking. Learners cannot prepare for real-life outcomes without analyzing, synthesizing and evaluating diverse perspectives. To practice critical thinking, we ask learners to identify and attempt to resolve *issues* that relate to the outcomes in real-life roles.

Figure 8, on the following page, shows some major issues a learner must

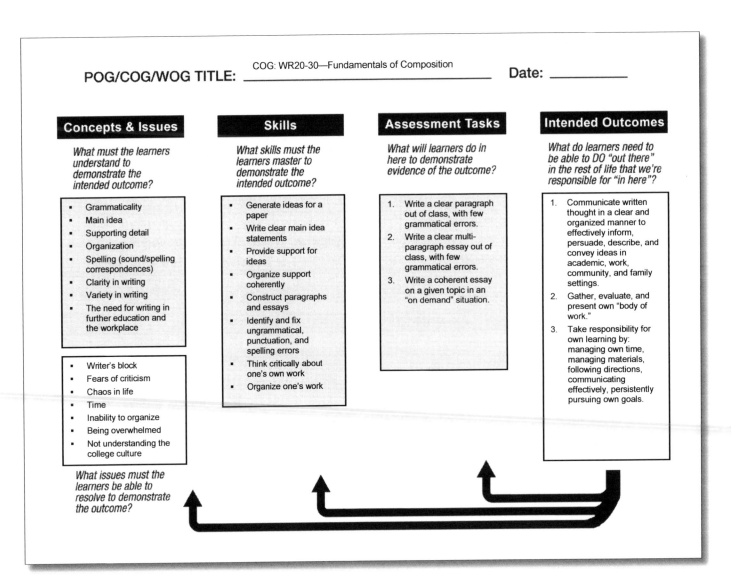

POG/COG/WOG TITLE: COG: WR20-30—Fundamentals of Composition _____ **Date:** _____

Concepts & Issues

What must the learners understand to demonstrate the intended outcome?

- Grammaticality
- Main idea
- Supporting detail
- Organization
- Spelling (sound/spelling correspondences)
- Clarity in writing
- Variety in writing
- The need for writing in further education and the workplace

- Writer's block
- Fears of criticism
- Chaos in life
- Time
- Inability to organize
- Being overwhelmed
- Not understanding the college culture

What issues must the learners be able to resolve to demonstrate the outcome?

Skills

What skills must the learners master to demonstrate the intended outcome?

- Generate ideas for a paper
- Write clear main idea statements
- Provide support for ideas
- Organize support coherently
- Construct paragraphs and essays
- Identify and fix ungrammatical, punctuation, and spelling errors
- Think critically about one's own work
- Organize one's work

Assessment Tasks

What will learners do in here to demonstrate evidence of the outcome?

1. Write a clear paragraph out of class, with few grammatical errors.
2. Write a clear multi-paragraph essay out of class, with few grammatical errors.
3. Write a coherent essay on a given topic in an "on demand" situation.

Intended Outcomes

What do learners need to be able to DO "out there" in the rest of life that we're responsible for "in here"?

1. Communicate written thought in a clear and organized manner to effectively inform, persuade, describe, and convey ideas in academic, work, community, and family settings.
2. Gather, evaluate, and present own "body of work."
3. Take responsibility for own learning by: managing own time, managing materials, following directions, communicating effectively, persistently pursuing own goals.

Figure 8: Issues in WR20–30, Fundamentals of Composition

The CONTENT Primer: Aligning Essential Content with Learning Outcomes

resolve when faced with writing, be that an essay, a report, a response to a letter or request, to mention a few.

So, the question we asked about *concepts* resurfaces about *issues*: How many *issues* will you include on the outcome guide for a program, course, or workshop?

All we can say is that depending on the level of complexity, working with i*ssues* can take a good deal of time. We might say they need their own *half-acre*.

What Skills Must Your Learners Develop?

Skills are most easily defined by how learners *develop* them. A learner develops *skills* through a routine of practice and feedback. The primary way we distinguish *skills* from *concepts* and *issues* is by the way skills are learned. A *skill* is developed using specific means and methods: demonstration, practice, feedback and more practice.

Think about how you learned to ride a bicycle. Understanding the concept of balance and resolving the issue of safety, while important, didn't enable you to ride the bike. You could have studied the concept of biking and the issues involved in biking and still not have been able to even balance on a bike. There are two simple things that tell you something needs to be taught (learned) as a skill:

- You know it will require demonstration, practice and feedback, and
- It is best described with an action phrase: ride a bicycle, think critically, communicate therapeutically.

Identifying the essential *skills* that are embedded in an outcome statement is a challenging part of an outcome-based curriculum design. There are macro *skills* and micro *skills* of every type. *Skills* can be as specific (micro) as writing a resume, listening actively, creating a graphic, using a computer program, giving an injection, or even mixing drinks. Technical (micro) skills make up much of the training that occurs in the workplace and career and technical education programs. (*Micro skills* are also referred to as competencies in the literature).

Skills can also be as broad (macro) as thinking systemically, collaborating with others, promoting wellness, negotiating contracts, advocating for a cause. All of these involve a complex set of *skills* that can be learned through demonstration, practice and feedback.

Figure 9, page 39, shows the essential skills needed by learners to achieve the intended learning outcomes in a composition/writing course.

One of the questions we get most often about listing skills on the one-page Outcome Guide template is about how specific we should be. We are often asked, "How far do we break them down?" Our answer is always that it is appropriate in a program, course, or workshop to identify *skill sets,* keeping them fairly general. Then, when we design learning activities we reduce the *skill set* to finer performance criteria that can be demonstrated and practiced.

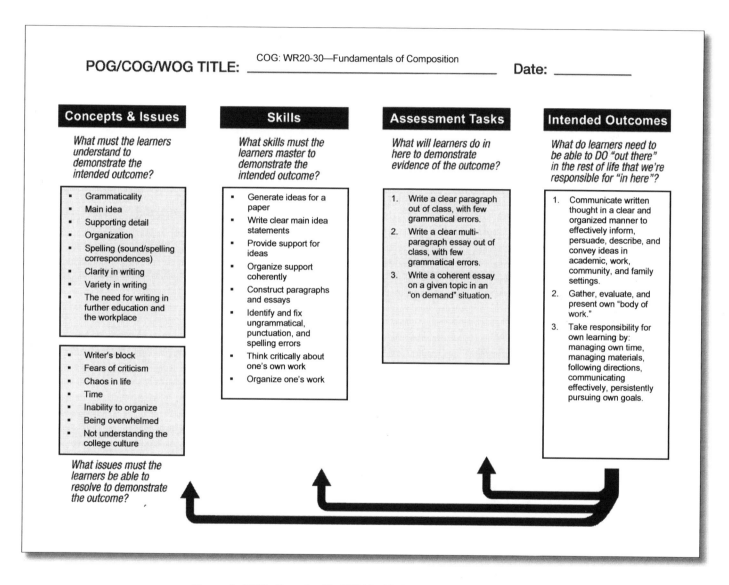

POG/COG/WOG TITLE: COG: WR20-30—Fundamentals of Composition

Date: _____

Concepts & Issues

What must the learners understand to demonstrate the intended outcome?

- Grammaticality
- Main idea
- Supporting detail
- Organization
- Spelling (sound/spelling correspondences)
- Clarity in writing
- Variety in writing
- The need for writing in further education and the workplace

- Writer's block
- Fears of criticism
- Chaos in life
- Time
- Inability to organize
- Being overwhelmed
- Not understanding the college culture

What issues must the learners be able to resolve to demonstrate the outcome?

Skills

What skills must the learners master to demonstrate the intended outcome?

- Generate ideas for a paper
- Write clear main idea statements
- Provide support for ideas
- Organize support coherently
- Construct paragraphs and essays
- Identify and fix ungrammatical, punctuation, and spelling errors
- Think critically about one's own work
- Organize one's work

Assessment Tasks

What will learners do in here to demonstrate evidence of the outcome?

1. Write a clear paragraph out of class, with few grammatical errors.
2. Write a clear multi-paragraph essay out of class, with few grammatical errors.
3. Write a coherent essay on a given topic in an "on demand" situation.

Intended Outcomes

What do learners need to be able to DO "out there" in the rest of life that we're responsible for "in here"?

1. Communicate written thought in a clear and organized manner to effectively inform, persuade, describe, and convey ideas in academic, work, community, and family settings.
2. Gather, evaluate, and present own "body of work."
3. Take responsibility for own learning by: managing own time, managing materials, following directions, communicating effectively, persistently pursuing own goals.

Figure 9: Skills Required in WR20–30, Fundamentals of Composition

Figure 10, below, is an example from our (Michele's) nursing program illustrating backwards design of a *skill set*. *Skills* become more detailed as we move from program to course to learning activity levels.

When comparing program, course and workshop designs, the number of *concepts, issues, and skills* that you list will vary a great deal depending on the intended learning outcomes. It is possible that the intended outcomes for a program of studies may call for a concentration of new *skills* development, while in a short workshop the need is to learn to resolve an *issue*, and at the course level, the major focus might be a thorough understanding of *concepts*. In most learning experiences, however, learning will be guided by a composite of *skills, concepts and issues* which are inherent in the learning outcomes.

Here's a question: You are teaching a course where *systems thinking* is a major focus. Given what you have learned about *concepts, issues and skills*, what is *systems thinking*? Is it a *concept, issue or skill*? Be careful!

Activity/Session Level	Course Level	Program Level
Prepare and administer a subcutaneous injection.	Administer oral, injectable and intravenous medications.	Interact with patients by engaging in safe, effective, quality nursing care and practices.

Figure 10: Backwards Design: Skill Set Examples across Design Levels

If your answer is a *concept*, you are right.

If your answer is an *issue*, you are right, also.

If your answer is a *skill,* you are right, again.

But how can this be? How can *systems thinking* be all three? Answer: It depends on what you are expecting the learners to do with it as it relates to your learning outcomes.

–If your intent in this course is for them to understand what *systems thinking* is conceptually, then you help them build that *concept* through reading and dialogue.

–If you want them to recognize the lack of *systems thinking* in our society, then you teach it as an *issue* they must try to resolve in the context of real-life situations. Of course, they will have to understand the concept first.

–But if you want the learner to actually think *systemically,* you have to intentionally break down the *skill* and teach it through demonstration, practice, and feedback repetitions.

Take a look at Figure 11 on the following page. It shows the *Course Outcome Guide* for a course on systemic thinking. Could this be enough to describe the essence of what must be learned, or do you find other *concepts, issues or skills* that need to be learned? Think about the intended outcome. Are there other *issues* that we haven't listed? Might this be enough as a basic structure for the course? You decide.

POG/COG/WOG TITLE: COG: Systemic Thinking   **Date:** _____

Concepts & Issues	Skills	Assessment Tasks	Intended Outcomes
What must the learners understand to demonstrate the intended outcome?	*What skills must the learners master to demonstrate the intended outcome?*	*What will learners do in here to demonstrate evidence of the outcome?*	*What do learners need to be able to DO "out there" in the rest of life that we're responsible for "in here"?*
▪ Systems ▪ Sustainability	▪ Apply a systemic process to planning ▪ Guide a committee through a systemic planning process that considers the systemic and sustainability needs of the community.	Conduct a mock committee meeting arriving at a systemic and sustainable proposal for one identified community need.	Guide a committee through a systemic planning process that considers the systemic and sustainability needs of the community.
▪ The lack of systems thinking in community planning			

What issues must the learners be able to resolve to demonstrate the outcome?

Figure 11: Course Outcome Guide: Systems Thinking

What Does a Good Outcome Guide Look Like?

The Central Oregon Community College Nursing Program has fully developed program, course and lab *outcome guides*. These guides have provided stability for a complex course of study and a platform for ongoing curriculum revision and assessment. Take a look at a sample of the Nursing *outcome guides* on the following pages and note the backwards design. Figure 12a is the *outcome guide* emphasizing the learning outcomes and essential content for a program of studies in Nursing. Figure 12b shows the learning outcomes and essential content for one of the courses in the Nursing program, Nursing II (NUR 107). Figure 12c shows Nursing Lab II related to NUR 107. Finally, Figure 12d shows learning outcomes and the essential content for the learning module, Administering Oral and Subcutaneous Medications, also related to Nursing 107.

Our team of outcome strategists have also provided several examples of *outcome guides* at the program, course and workshop levels for college, community and workplace settings. These can be found in Appendix A.

So, now is your chance to identify (or maybe re-assess) the essential content for a course you plan to deliver, or are currently teaching.

POG/COG/WOG TITLE: _____ POG: Associate of Applied Science (AAS) Degree in Nursing _____ **Date:** _____

Concepts & Issues	**Skills**	**Assessment Tasks**	**Intended Outcomes**
What must the learners understand to demonstrate the intended outcome?	*What skills must the learners master to demonstrate the intended outcome?*	*What will learners do in here to demonstrate evidence of the outcome?*	*What do learners need to be able to DO "out there" in the rest of life that we're responsible for "in here"?*

Concepts & Issues

Biophysical Concepts:
-Physiological Systems
Psychosocial Concepts:
-Mental Health
Reproductive Concepts:
-Women's Health
-Men's Health
-Childbearing
Nursing Domain Concepts:
-Nursing Process
-Patient Care
-Clinical Decision Making
Healthcare Domain Concept:
-Systems
-Safety
-Quality

- Access to healthcare
- Changing practice
- Complex needs of an aging society
- Cultural competence
- End of life care
- High patient acuity

What issues must the learners be able to resolve to demonstrate the outcome?

Skills

- Perform a complete set of nursing skills to provide safe, effective, quality nursing care
- Provide holistic, individualized patient care based on the nursing process across the lifespan and in various care settings
- Maintain accountability, confidentiality and integrity in nursing practice
- Make clinical decisions based on established legal, ethical and professional standards, and evidence based practice

Assessment Tasks

1. Using a nurse-mentor (preceptor) model and specific performance criteria, the learner will demonstrate delivery of patient care in five major nursing roles: health promotion and care delivery, care management, learning and teaching, professional relationships and quality care advocacy.
2. Given a patient-centered case study, produce a plan of nursing care supported by scientific rationale.
3. Given a healthcare-related ethical dilemma, arrive at a solution founded on medical/nursing ethical theory and practice.

Intended Outcomes

1. Apply the nursing process to provide individualized, safe and effective patient care in acute, critical, community based and long-term care settings.
2. Coordinate, manage and utilize professional communication skills to meet the health care needs for a group of patients across the continuum of practice settings.
3. Develop and implement individualized teaching plans for patients, families, and caregivers.
4. Internalize and model professional behaviors and values within the scope of practice of the registered nurse.
5. Integrates systematic and continuous actions to promote measurable improvement in patient care.

Figure 12a: Program Outcome Guide (POG): Nursing

POG/COG/WOG TITLE: _____ Date: _____

COG: Nursing 107: Nursing II

Concepts & Issues	Skills	Assessment Tasks	Intended Outcomes
What must the learners understand to demonstrate the intended outcome?	*What skills must the learners master to demonstrate the intended outcome?*	*What will learners do in here to demonstrate evidence of the outcome?*	*What do learners need to be able to DO "out there" in the rest of life that we're responsible for "in here"?*
Biophysical Concepts: Fluids and Electrolytes, Infection, Metabolism, Oxygenation, Perfusion, Tissue Integrity *Nursing Domain Concepts:* Clinical Decision Making, Communication, Teaching and Learning *Healthcare Domain Concept:* Accountability, Evidence-based Practice, Quality Improvement	• Integrate skill set in the performance of case-based lab activities and patient care • Use critical thinking skills in making clinical decisions • Grow professionally through reflective practice	1. Given a patient situation, simulate the delivery of nursing care including: • Patient assessment • Medication administration • Patient teaching regarding medications • Urinary catheterization 2. Using a clinical model, the faculty will observe the learner in the planning and delivery of patient care as defined by specific performance criteria pertaining to the NUR 107 level nursing roles. 3. Given a surgical procedure, produce a patient teaching brochure.	1. Apply the assessment and intervention steps of the nursing process in the implementation of care for two patients based on established standards of care. 2. Communicate therapeutically and professionally with patients and families 3. Identify patient learning needs and reinforce patient teaching from established standard. 4. Apply professional behaviors as a member of the healthcare team. 5. Provide basic nursing care based on ethical/legal principles.

• Safe clinical environment
• End of life care
• Ineffective communication

What issues must the learners be able to resolve to demonstrate the outcome?

Figure 12b: Course Outcome Guide (COG): Nursing 107

POG/COG/WOG TITLE: _____ COG: Nursing 107: Nursing II, Lab Section _____   **Date:** _____

Concepts & Issues	**Skills**	**Assessment Tasks**	**Intended Outcomes**
What must the learners understand to demonstrate the intended outcome?	*What skills must the learners master to demonstrate the intended outcome?*	*What will learners do in here to demonstrate evidence of the outcome?*	*What do learners need to be able to DO "out there" in the rest of life that we're responsible for "in here"?*

Biophysical Concepts:
- Comfort
- Fluids and Electrolytes
- Infection
- Perfusion
- Tissue Integrity

Nursing Domain Concepts:
- Assessment
- Caring Interventions
- Communication
- Managing Care

Healthcare Domain Concept:
- Evidence-based Practice

- Proper patient identification
- Medical and Nursing errors
- Hospital acquired infection

What issues must the learners be able to resolve to demonstrate the outcome?

Skills column:

- Administer oral, injectable and parenteral medications:
  - Oral
  - Intramuscular injection
  - Subcutaneous injection
  - Intradermal injection
  - Mixed insulin injection
  - IV piggyback
- Administer intravenous fluid:
  - IV site assessment
  - Priming tubing
  - Fluids by gravity and pump
- Perform sterile procedures:
  - Urinary catheter insertion with sterile gloving
  - Sterile/complex dressings

Assessment Tasks column:

1. Given patient situations, meet or exceed outcome criteria for skills performance checklists for all check-offs.
2. Given a case scenario, meet or exceed outcome criteria for the comprehensive assessment.
3. Pass medication math exam at >90%.

Intended Outcomes column:

1. Administer medications and parenteral fluids following the six rights and three check rules of safe medication administration.
2. Perform sterile procedures maintaining asepsis.
3. Organize and perform steps of skill to promote efficiency, safety, and patient comfort.
4. Document care delivery on appropriate flow sheets and narrative patient care notes.

Figure 12c: Course Outcome Guide (COG): Nursing Lab 107

POG/COG/WOG TITLE: COG: Administering Oral and Subcutaneous Medications _____ **Date:** _____

Concepts & Issues

What must the learners understand to demonstrate the intended outcome?

Biophysical Concepts:
Infection

Nursing Domain Concepts:
Caring Interventions
Communication
Teaching and Learning

Healthcare Domain Concept:
Safety

- Safe clinical environment
- Medical and Nursing Errors

Skills

What skills must the learners master to demonstrate the intended outcome?

- Calculate a prescribed medication dosage
- Determine medications that can and cannot be crushed
- Split and crush oral tablets
- Measure and administer liquid medications
- Maintain aseptic technique during the administration of a parenteral medication
- Prepare and administer a subcutaneous injection

Assessment Tasks

What will learners do in here to demonstrate evidence of the outcome?

Given a simple patient case study scenario, simulate the safe administration of oral and subcutaneous medications according to given and defined performance criteria.

Intended Outcomes

What do learners need to be able to DO "out there" in the rest of life that we're responsible for "in here"?

1. Prepare and administer oral and subcutaneous medications according to guidelines for safe medication delivery.
2. Document medication administration according to national and facility standards.
3. Administer medications following legal principles.
4. Practice according to the six rights and three checks of safe medication administration.

What issues must the learners be able to resolve to demonstrate the outcome?

Figure 12d: Outcome Guide: Admistering Oral and Subcutaneous Medications

The next section, *Determining Essential Content: A Facilitator's Guide*, is a step-by-step process to help you determine the essential content for a course you are teaching or will teach. It is advisable to request the assistance of a small group of colleagues through this process as a way to develop objectively the essential content for a course. It can also be adapted for determining essential content for a program of studies and for workshops or trainings. The only two things you need to get started are:

1) a list of carefully formulated learning outcome statements and

2) a few experts in the content area to assist you.

Determining Essential Content: A Facilitator's Guide

Purpose

The purpose of this guide is to identify essential content in the design of an outcome-based program, course, workshop or training. It does not include instructions for generating learning outcomes; you will find those instructions in the facilitator's guide section of *The OUTCOME Primer: Envisioning Learning Outcomes*. Neither does it include instructions for identifying appropriate assessment tasks; you will find those instructions in the facilitator's guide section of *The ASSESSMENT Primer: Assessing and Tracking Evidence of Learning Outcomes*. Both Primers have been referenced in prior sections of this book.

Here in this Facilitator's Guide of *The CONTENT Primer: Aligning Essential Content with Learning Outcomes*, you will learn a step-by-step process for identifying the essential content (*concepts, issues, skills*) required of learners to demonstrate the intended learning outcomes in programs, courses and workshops. *The process explained here focuses on determining the essential content at the course level, but it is easily adapted at the program and workshop levels.*

Overview of the Process

In keeping with our deep belief that curriculum building is really an on-going conversation, the process we describe here is a way to focus that conversation. By its very nature, a conversation involves other participants to assist you in identifying here the essential content for a course that will be transferred onto a one page template, the *Course Outcome Guide* (COG), described previously in Part Three, page 29.

Participants

When working at the course outcome (COG) level, you will benefit by involving 4–6 participants including those who have taught the course as well as others who have different perspectives on the course. Faculty are the content experts with a wealth of information. It is important to have outside participants involved in at least the first part of this session.

Preparation Prior to the Work Session

1. ***Choose participants with diverse perspectives.*** In addition to designated instructors, be sure to invite person(s) who have a first-hand view of the role(s) for which the learners are being prepared in this course. (In a college program you may already have an advisory group that fits this purpose.) What you need are persons who have diverse insights into what knowledge and skills are essential to the intended outcomes. As stated above, 4–6 persons are optimal. More than 6 persons become difficult, but not impossible. While you can follow this process alone, it is not advisable.

    In addition to giving participants the time, place and length of this work session (1–2 hours), tell them why they are important to this process. Their contribution will be greater if they know their expertise is unique.

2. ***Prepare yourself.*** Review your understanding of the content elements (concepts, issues, skills) in the previous sections of this Primer. Furthermore, re-assess your outcome statements against the criteria in Figure 2: Scoring Guide-Assessing the Quality of Intended Outcome Statements on page 7 of this Primer, making sure they are clear and robust statements.

3. ***Decide where to start: concepts, issues or skills.*** As you analyze the learning outcomes to determine the essential content, decide whether *concepts, issues,* or *skills* will be your initial focus. Begin with the one you think will be most prominent. If none of the *concepts*, *issues*, or *skills* seem prominent, begin with *concepts*, which we have done here.

4. ***Prepare the materials.*** *(Put your computer away. You need paper, pencil and good eye contact.)*

   • Make copies of the worksheets on pages 61–64 for each person assisting you. You may want to enlarge them to poster or flip chart size if you are working with more than 4 persons.

   • Print the course's learning outcome statements on a flip chart sheet large enough for everyone to see from a distance. Hang (or tape) it at the *far right* of the wall space. *The placement is important to the feeling of "designing-backward"* and reflects the outcome guide template, shown in Figure 5, page 29. In addition, have participants copy the outcome statements onto Figure 13, Learning Outcomes Worksheet, shown on page 61. (Optional: If program level outcome statements are available, post them to the far right of the course level outcomes.)

- (Optional) If you have identified the key assessment tasks (refer to *The ASSESSMENT Primer: Assessing and Tracking Evidence of Learning Outcomes*) print and post them next to and left of the outcome statements. This layout will continue the concept of designing backwards. Leave space on the left for three content flip charts, as suggested below.

- Write the following questions separately at the top of three flip chart papers and post them to the left of the flip chart containing the performance tasks and learning outcome statements:

  Concepts: *What concepts will the learners need to understand in order to demonstrate the intended learning outcome?*

  Issues: *What issues will the learners need to be able to resolve in order to demonstrate the intended learning outcome?*

  Skills: *What skills will the learners need to develop in order to demonstrate the intended learning outcome?*

- Gather a flip chart pad, easel, and markers. Gather additional materials: Super-sticky Post-it® Notes, 3x3 inches in size are best; masking tape (unless you have self-adhesive flip chart sheets); fine point black markers for each participant.

  (Optional) Collect and have ready any clustered Post-it® Notes that you retained from your outcomes work session, when learning outcomes were previously established *(described in PART THREE, Developing Significant Outcomes: A Facilitator's Guide of The OUTCOMES Primer: Envisioning Learning Outcomes)*.

Facilitate the Work Session   Time: 1–2 hours

1. **Start the work session**
   - Ask everyone to take a seat at the tables.

   - Introduce yourself and talk briefly about the purpose of the work session.

   - Acknowledge the different participants and what each brings to this work.

   - Explain the three content building blocks and how they differ.

     ○ Concepts: Major ideas the learners need to understand, usually expressed in as little as 1–3 words.

     ○ Issues: Problems or concerns the learners need to identify and seek to resolve.

     ○ Skills: Specific tasks the learners need to be able to do which are mastered through practice and feedback expressed as action statements.

   - Draw the figure on the next page on a flipchart. Talk about where concepts, issues and skills come from.

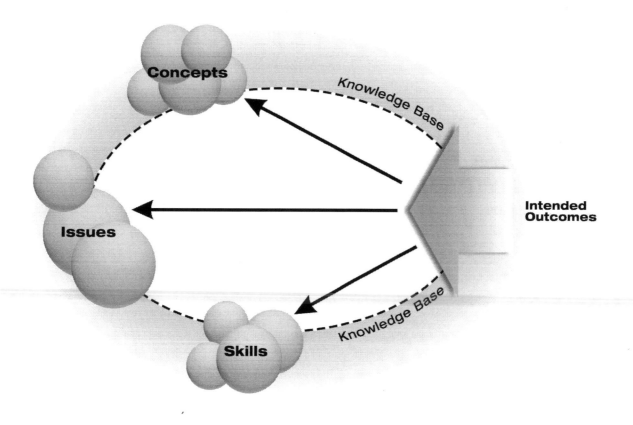

2. ***Get ready to brainstorm!***

- Move the flip chart paper with the first content question, below, in front of participants where all can see.

- Read aloud the following question: "What **concepts** will the learners need to understand in order to demonstrate the intended learning outcome?"

- ***Read or Post the Rules** for Brainstorming:*

    - <u>Answer</u> the question independently and silently. (Don't discuss your answers yet!)

    - <u>Think</u> about the concepts the learners need to understand in order to demonstrate the intended outcome(s).

    - <u>Write</u> one answer per Post-it® Note using the black marker—no pens please since they are harder for everyone to see.

    - <u>Use</u> 1–3 words to describe the concept. It is not necessary to start with an action word for concepts and issues, just for skills.

    - <u>Create</u> as many Post-it® Notes as you can!

3. **Get ready to post!**

    - *__Give these Instructions__—Posting (5–10 minutes):*

        ○ <u>Collect</u> all of your Post-it® Notes.

        ○ <u>Form</u> a semi-circle around the posting area, where the flip chart re-sides.

        ○ <u>Have each person read</u> one answer out loud and have them post on the white board/ flip chart.

            • One person at a time, one answer at a time until all answers are exhausted.

        ○ <u>Discard</u> any answers already posted (duplicates).

        ○ <u>Create</u> more Post-it® Notes as new answers occur to you and others.

        ○ <u>Continue</u> to post until Post-it® Notes are exhausted. (Known as brain-drain!)

4. **Reach consensus**

    - <u>Discuss the items on the flipchart</u>. Talk all you want—this is the collaborative process!

    - <u>Set aside</u> left-overs that don't seem to fit anywhere.

    - <u>Work until you have consensus</u> on which items are the essential concepts, from simpler to complex.

- Transfer the essential *concepts* onto Figure 14, Concepts and Issues Worksheet, on page 62.

Repeat the above process to determine issues and skills:

What __issues__ will the learners need to be able to resolve in order to demonstrate the intended learning outcome(s)?

What __skills__ will the learners need to develop in order to demonstrate the intended learning outcome(s)? (Remember, skills are written as action statements, e.g. think systemically, administer medications. Make sure skills start with an action word.)

(Note: When brain-storming ideas for issues and skills, use respective work-sheets, shown on pages 62 and 63.)

Summarize and Ask the "Big Question"

1. ***Ask this question:*** *When you think you have captured the essential concepts, issues and skills for a course, ask this important question.*

   "If the learner understands these concepts (read them out loud) **and resolve these issues** (read them out loud) **and can demonstrate these skills** (read them out loud), **are these sufficient for them to achieve these intended learning outcomes?"**

2. **Respond to the question:** Ask everyone to share their responses to the above question. Make any revisions to the listed concepts, issues and skills on the flip chart paper (or worksheets on pages 61–63).

Complete a first draft of a Course Outcome Guide

1. **Create first draft:** (Important) Tell the participants you'll put together a draft of the COG template, as described and shown on page 29, for them to review

    Using the flipcharts (or handouts) containing the essential content (concepts, issues, and skills) from the earlier brainstorming process, write in the learning outcome statements and the listing of items under each of the three components for essential content onto the Course Outcome Guide (COG) template. Take license with the wording, keeping terms parallel and list words in an order that makes sense to you. (In many cases, you will leave the column, Performance Tasks, empty if you have not conducted a process for analyzing the performance task(s) as described in *The ASSESSMENT Primer: Assessing and Tracking Evidence of Learning Outcomes*.)

2. **Send first/initial draft and ask for review:** Send the initial copy of the COG template to all participants asking for their review. You may ask them if they wish to have this template sent to them through email or other media rather than having another formal meeting.

    Attach any notes with questions you have that may trigger some revision.

    Include a copy of the Scoring Guide for Content Descriptions (page 64) and ask participants to return comments and suggestions back to you. Include a time (day, month) when all reviews are due.

    Note: It is important to get the first draft of the Outcome Guide containing the essential content to the participants as soon as possible for their review.

3. **Triangulate:** While you are waiting for participants' reviews, proceed with the following:

   - Investigate whether essential content reflects contemporary literature and practice trends.

   - Explore other educational programs or courses with similar outcomes for prevailing concepts, issues and skills, and compare.

   - Reflect and analyze other professional organizations' curricula for alignment with your identified essential content.

4. **Compile reviews and assessments:** Collect all reviews from participants and merge with the results of your assessment conducted through the triangulation process in #3 above.

   Add or delete any items of the essential content and record on the Outcome Guide (COG) Template. Most importantly, confirm that the selected concepts, issues, and skills, decided upon, connect to your identified learning outcomes.

Final Steps

1. **Complete the Course Outcome Guide (COG)**
   Complete a finished version of all essential content (concepts, issues, and skills) as a result of the above processes and transfer on to a final version of the Course Outcome Guide.

2. **Distribute the Course Outcome Guide (COG)**
   Distribute the COG to all participants who have assisted you in this conversational process.

3. **Thank the participants**

   Your role as facilitator for this session is now finished. Thank the participants for their input and efforts.

Learning Outcomes

What do learners need to be able to do "out there" that we're responsible for "in here"?

1. _____

2. _____

3. _____

4. _____

5. _____

6. _____

7. _____

8. _____

Note: "Out there" refers to the many roles learners fill in the rest of their lives beyond this course (or program or workshop), including being a successful student in the next course(s).

"In here" refers to just in this course (or program or workshop).

There are usually no more than 1–4 outcome statements per course and no more than 6–8 outcome statements in a program of studies. A PDF version of this page is included on our web page, *www.outcomeprimers.com*, for your use.

Figure 13: Learning Outcomes Worksheet

Concepts & Issues

Concepts

What must learners understand to demonstrate the intended outcomes?

- _____
- _____
- _____
- _____
- _____
- _____
- _____
- _____
- _____
- _____
- _____
- _____
- _____
- _____
- _____

Issues

What issues must learners be able to resolve to demonstrate the outcome?

- _____
- _____
- _____
- _____
- _____
- _____
- _____
- _____
- _____
- _____
- _____
- _____
- _____
- _____
- _____

Note: A concept or issue can usually be represented by one to three words. A PDF version of this page is included on our web page, _www.outcomeprimers.com_, for your use.

Figure 14: Concepts and Issues Worksheet

Skills

What skills must the learner master to demonstrate the intended outcome?

- _____

- _____

- _____

- _____

- _____

- _____

- _____

- _____

- _____

- _____

Note: Skills are abilities developed through demonstration and repetitions of practice and feedback. A PDF version of this page is on our web page, *www.outcomeprimers.com*, for your use.

Figure 15: Skills Worksheet

Scoring Guide for Content Descriptions

Use this rating to assess your Content Descriptions
1=absent   2=developing   3=adequate   4=well developed

Characteristics of Good Content Descriptions					Additional comments and specific suggestions for improvement
1. Concepts	1	2	3	4	
Consists of key words or phrases that describe the essential ideas about which the students must discover some depth of meaning in order to achieve the intended outcomes (8–15 is usually sufficient).					
2. Issues	1	2	3	4	
Consists of the key problems learners must work to resolve, which are inherent in the intended outcomes (usually no more than 4–5).					
3. Skills	1	2	3	4	
Consists of action statements which describe abilities that are essential to demonstrate the intended outcomes (usually no more than 8).					

Figure 16: Scoring Guide for Content Descriptions

PART FOUR
Continuing Your Learning

"Tell me, and I will forget. Show me, and I may remember.
Involve me, and I will understand."

—Confucius, 450 BC

Continuing Your Learning

In Conclusion

In *The CONTENT Primer: Aligning Essential Content with Learning Outcomes*, you have learned the process of analyzing learning outcomes to determine the essential content of a program, course or workshop. You have also learned the importance of moving away from topics towards identifying *essential content* in the form of *concepts, issues and skills*, all of which can be displayed on a one-page template, the Outcome Guide, Figure 5, page 29.

You can now let go of the guilt forcing you and the rest of us instructors to constantly try to *cover everything* and rejoice in guiding our students towards essential content.

Next Steps

In this book of *The OUTCOME Primers Series 2.0*, we have limited our discussion to analyzing learning outcomes to determine essential content for programs, courses and workshops. **The** *CONTENT Primer: Aligning Essential Content with Learning Outcomes* adds to the continuing process of outcome-based curriculum design.

It is our hope that working through this book has helped build your capacity to:

Work to identify, delimit and align essential content with learning outcomes by *designing backwards, outside in*; design programs, courses and workshops from a contemporary, constructivist understanding of learning.

We encourage you to further your learning in each of the other books of *The OUTCOME Primers Series 2.0*. The intended learning outcomes for each of the other Primers in this series are described here.

The OUTCOME Primer: Envisioning Learning Outcomes, *Stiehl and Sours*

Working through this book should help build your capacity to:

Envision and develop concise and robust learning outcome statements that are relevant to life roles and drive essential content and assessment in training and educational programs; help others understand learning outcomes as essential for effective instruction.

The ASSESSMENT Primer: Assessing and Tracking Evidence of Learning Outcomes, *Stiehl and Null*

Working through this book should help build your capacity to:

Develop tasks, tools and systemic processes for assessing and tracking evidence of learning outcomes to assist and advance learners and continuously improve learning experiences (at the course, program and organization levels).

The MAPPING Primer: Mapping The Way to Learning Outcomes, *Stiehl and Telban*

Working through this book should help build your capacity to:

- Create a visual map of learning experiences in programs and courses;
- Facilitate mapping sessions to align outcomes, improve sequencing, and use resources to achieve intended learning outcomes.

The GUIDING Primer: Guiding Toward Learning Outcomes, *Prickel and Stiehl*

Working through this book should help build your capacity to:

Move beyond the old-school perception of what it means to *teach* to *guiding* learners using eight essential instructional practices in the pursuit of intended learning outcomes.

The SUSTAINABILITY Primer:
Sustaining Learning Outcomes and
Assessment, *Stiehl and Telban*

Working through this book should help build your capacity to:

Create and sustain an outcomes and assessment system through effective leadership, instructor involvement, professional development, and system integration.

Appendix A: Sample POGs, COGs, and WOGs

The following examples highlight the essential content of various programs, courses, workshops and trainings.

Program Outcome Guides (POG): EXAMPLES

Course Outcome Guides (COG): EXAMPLES

Workshop Outcome Guides (WOG): EXAMPLES

POG/COG/WOG TITLE: POG: Adult Instructional Systems: Masters Degree in Education EdM

Date: _____

Concepts & Issues

What must the learners understand to demonstrate the intended outcome?

- Learning and learning theory
- Instructional strategies
- Learning organization
- Assessment
- Outcome-based learning
- Curricular design
- Systems thinking
- Learner-centered instruction
- Paradigms/frameworks
- Intended outcomes
- Assessment tasks
- Backwards design
- Inside-out

- The implementation and sustainability of outcome-based learning across an organization.

What issues must the learners be able to resolve to demonstrate the outcome?

Skills

What skills must the learners master to demonstrate the intended outcome?

- Construct a profile of one's own adult development.
- Apply learning theories to one's own teaching and learning philosophy.
- Conduct learning needs assessments.
- Use current and emerging technologies to research current and emerging trends in education.
- Design an internship project.
- Design instructional systems that are driven by intended learning outcomes.
- Create effective assessment tasks.
- Use current and emerging technologies.

Assessment Tasks

What will learners do in here to demonstrate evidence of the outcome?

Construct a professional portfolio that includes:

1. Learning outcomes and assessment tasks for an academic or training program.
2. A personal philosophy of teaching and learning based on learning theory.
3. A personal definition of leadership.
4. A description of critical incidents leading to one's growth and changes in the program.
5. An internship report including an analysis of results (pros and cons).
6. A critical analysis of four different products reflecting skills developed in this program.

Intended Outcomes

What do learners need to be able to DO "out there" in the rest of life that we're responsible for "in here"?

1. Apply practical instructional strategies based on a theoretical model of learning in education and workplace settings.
2. Promote the transformation of organizations into learning organizations.
3. Design and develop outcome-based learning systems to meet identified needs.
4. Systemically inquire into, and report on one's own professional practice.
5. Use emerging technology to support teaching and learning.

POG/COG/WOG TITLE: _____ POG: Associate of Applied Science (AAS) Degree in Nursing _____   **Date:** _____

Concepts & Issues	**Skills**	**Assessment Tasks**	**Intended Outcomes**
What must the learners understand to demonstrate the intended outcome?	*What skills must the learners master to demonstrate the intended outcome?*	*What will learners do in here to demonstrate evidence of the outcome?*	*What do learners need to be able to DO "out there" in the rest of life that we're responsible for "in here"?*
Biophysical -Physiological Systems **Psychosocial** -Mental Health **Reproductive** -Women's Health -Men's Health -Childbearing **Nursing Domain** -Nursing Process -Patient Care -Clinical Decision Making **Healthcare Domain** -Systems -Safety -Quality	▪ Perform a complete set of nursing skills to provide safe, effective, quality nursing care. ▪ Provide holistic, individualized patient care based on the nursing process across the lifespan and in various care settings. ▪ Maintain accountability, confidentiality and integrity in nursing practice. ▪ Make clinical decisions based on established legal, ethical and professional standards, and evidence based practice.	▪ Using a nurse-mentor (preceptor) model and specific performance criteria, the learner will demonstrate delivery of patient care in five major nursing roles: health promotion and care delivery, care management, learning and teaching, professional relationships and quality care advocacy. ▪ Given a patient-centered case study, produce a plan of nursing care supported by scientific rationale. ▪ Given a healthcare-related ethical dilemma, arrive at a solution founded on medical/nursing ethical theory and practice.	1. Apply the nursing process to provide individualized, safe and effective patient care in acute, critical, community based and long-term care settings. 2. Coordinate, manage and utilize professional communication skills to meet the health care needs for a group of patients across the continuum of practice settings. 3. Develop and implement individualized teaching plans for patients, families, and caregivers. 4. Internalize and model professional behaviors and values within the scope of practice of the registered nurse. 5. Integrates systematic and continuous actions to promote measurable improvement in patient care.

▪ Access to healthcare
▪ Changing practice
▪ Complex needs of an aging society
▪ Cultural competence
▪ End of life care
▪ High patient acuity

What issues must the learners be able to resolve to demonstrate the outcome?

POG/COG/WOG TITLE: POG: Dental Assistant Program _____ **Date:** _____

Concepts & Issues

What must the learners understand to demonstrate the intended outcome?

- Biomedical & clinical science Communication Confidentiality/Privacy
- Dental and medical emergencies
- Dental materials
- Dental practice related hazards General dentistry
- Infection control
- Legal/ethical principles Oral anatomy/histology/embryology
- Oral health & education
- Patient care
- Pharmacology
- Practice management Professionalism
- Quality care
- Radiology
- Safety (patient/occupational)

- Anxious/phobic patients
- Aspiration
- Bleeding
- Pain
- Medical emergencies

What issues must the learners be able to resolve to demonstrate the outcome?

Skills

What skills must the learners master to demonstrate the intended outcome?

- Adapt care to special needs patients
- Assist in dental procedures
- Assist chairside emergencies
- Calculate ratios/percentage
- Communicate with patients and dental team
- Implement radiographic procedures
- Manage pain and anxiety using non-pharmacological measures
- Manage patient records
- Operate and maintain dental equipment
- Participate in business office procedures
- Perform according to EFDA & Oregon Board of Dentistry guides
- Perform intake skills
- Protect patients and self from harm
- Teach patients

Assessment Tasks

What will learners do in here to demonstrate evidence of the outcome?

1. Given a simulated patient care scenario, demonstrate a dental assisting skill set for a dental surgery procedure.
2. As part of patient care delivery in a dental office, document care provided according to established performance criteria.
3. Using an observation/performance assessment model using defined performance criteria by faculty, demonstrate the planning and delivery of dental office skills in the role of a dental assistant.

Intended Outcomes

What do learners need to be able to DO "out there" in the rest of life that we're responsible for "in here"?

1. Exercise safe practices and personal care to all patients consistent with current and emerging principles of biomedical, dental, clinical and behavioral sciences.
2. Document the dental treatments of patients to facilitate continuity and safe patient care.
3. Maintain records of the dental practice in compliance with state/federal laws and the Oregon Board of Dentistry.
4. Act accountably and with integrity in all personal and professional matters.
5. Engage interpersonally and professionally with patients and dental co-workers and practitioners.

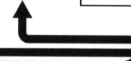

POG/COG/WOG TITLE: POG: Associate of Science (AS) Degree and Certificate Program—Paralegal Studies

Date: _____

Concepts & Issues

What must the learners understand to demonstrate the intended outcome?

- Legality
- Advocacy
- Laws: Constitutional, Statutory, Judicial, Administrative, Case
- Plaintiff
- Defendant
- Jury
- Communication
- Plea
- Plea bargaining
- Federal & State Systems
- Civil
- Criminal
- Case
- Ethics

- Arguing according to current law
- Ethical actions
- Client advocacy

What issues must the learners be able to resolve to demonstrate the outcome?

Skills

What skills must the learners master to demonstrate the intended outcome?

- Use legal software
- Find and recognize relevant facts
- Conduct computer searches
- Identify legal issues and law in particular to case at hand
- Obtain legal documents from appropriate authority
- Organize documents and other evidence
- Shepardize {is law still current?}
- Identify and find current law
- Spot issues {analyze a legal issue}
- Think critically
- Analyze laws
- Think originally and independently
- Represent others
- Communicate orally
- Write in legal format

Assessment Tasks

What will learners do in here to demonstrate evidence of the outcome?

1. Prepare and write legal briefs and memoranda appropriate for presentation to a court or judge.
2. Prepare a case, using the different sources of law {constitutional, statutory, judicial, administrative} and legal procedures.
3. Research, organize and use {legal} resources for identifying the legal issues and laws pertaining to a case.
4. Advocate for and represent others ethically and intelligently consistent with legal procedures.
5. Provide written and/or verbal rationale and justification for specific laws pertaining to a case.

Intended Outcomes

What do learners need to be able to DO "out there" in the rest of life that we're responsible for "in here"?

1. Prepare and write legal briefs and memoranda appropriate for submission to the court/opposing party.
2. Use the different sources of law (Constitutional, Statutory, Case law, Administrative) in preparation for client's case.
3. Treat all cases, personnel, and clients in a sensitive, ethical and confidential manner.
4. Advocate for and represent others ethically and intelligently consistent with substantive and procedural law.
5. Provide written and/or verbal arguments, rationale, and justification for specific laws pertaining to a case.

POG/COG/WOG TITLE: _____ COG: AED531: Instructional Design **Date:** _____

Concepts & Issues	Skills	Assessment Tasks	Intended Outcomes
What must the learners understand to demonstrate the intended outcome?	*What skills must the learners master to demonstrate the intended outcome?*	*What will learners do in here to demonstrate evidence of the outcome?*	*What do learners need to be able to DO "out there" in the rest of life that we're responsible for "in here"?*

Concepts & Issues

- Curriculum frameworks
- Envisioning learning
- Systematic/systemic
- Open/closed systems
- Analysis/synthesis
- Both/and
- Systems thinking
- Zoom
- Boundaries; layers
- Self-organizing
- Feedback loops
- Disturbance/change
- Learning outcomes
- Process skills
- Performance tasks

- Learner-centered facilitation
- Criteria/scoring guides

What issues must the learners be able to resolve to demonstrate the outcome?

Skills

Program Level:
- Identify an instructional need
- Use interview, affinity group or focus group techniques
- State program outcomes clearly in performance terms -Design-down concepts and process skills from outcomes (POG)
- Identify performance tasks
- Create program maps

Course Level:
- Design-down the essential concepts and process skills for courses in the program
- Create a course COG
- Prepare a course syllabus/training guide
- Prepare scoring guides

Lesson/Activity Level:
- Plan learning activities for specific concepts or process skills that integrate the seven factors of learner success

Assessment Tasks

Level 1: Program Level
Design-down an outcome based instructional program (college or workplace) that includes:
-Tool 1: Outcome Detail
-Tool 2: Program Map
-Tool 3: Program Outcome Guide (POG)

Level 2: Course Level
Design-down an outcome based college course or training module that consists of Tool 2: Course Outcome Guide & Syllabus

Level 3: Instructional Level
Design an outcome-based learning experience (college or workplace) that addresses the factors of learner success.

Intended Outcomes

1. Use systemic and strategic thinking to design college curriculum and teaching in the context of the 21st Century (the Age of Paradox).

2. Use systemic and strategic thinking to create effective learning experiences in the high performance work place of the 21st Century.

POG/COG/WOG TITLE: _____ COG: Nursing 107: Nursing II _____ **Date:** _____

Concepts & Issues

What must the learners understand to demonstrate the intended outcome?

Biophysical Concepts:
Fluids and Electrolytes
Infection
Metabolism
Oxygenation
Perfusion
Tissue Integrity

Nursing Domain Concepts:
Clinical Decision Making
Communication
Teaching and Learning

Healthcare Concepts:
Accountability
Evidence-based Practice
Quality Improvement

- Safe clinical environment
- End of life care
- Ineffective communication

What issues must the learners be able to resolve to demonstrate the outcome?

Skills

What skills must the learners master to demonstrate the intended outcome?

- Integrate skill set in the performance of case-based lab activities and patient care.
- Use critical thinking skills in making clinical decisions.
- Grow professionally through reflective practice.

Assessment Tasks

What will learners do in here to demonstrate evidence of the outcome?

1. Given a patient situation, simulate the delivery of nursing care including:
   - Patient assessment
   - Medication administration
   - Patient teaching regarding medications
   - Urinary catheterization
2. Using a clinical model, the faculty will observe the learner in the planning and delivery of patient care as defined by specific performance criteria pertaining to the NUR 107 level nursing roles.
3. Given a surgical procedure, produce a patient teaching brochure.

Intended Outcomes

What do learners need to be able to DO "out there" in the rest of life that we're responsible for "in here"?

1. Apply the assessment and intervention steps of the nursing process in the implementation of care for two patients based on established standards of care.
2. Communicate therapeutically and professionally with patients and families.
3. Identify patient learning needs and reinforce patient teaching from established standards.
4. Apply professional behaviors as a member of the healthcare team.
5. Provide basic nursing care based on ethical/legal principles.

POG/COG/WOG TITLE: _COG: Cinema 112: Script Analysis_ Date: _____

Concepts & Issues

What must the learners understand to demonstrate the intended outcome?

- Production value
- Television
- Motion picture
- Logline
- Session
- Step out
- Mini reviews
- Grammatical conventions
- Coverage
- Beat sheet
- Film
- Synopsis
- Plot
- Analysis

- Plagiarism
- Confidentiality

What issues must the learners be able to resolve to demonstrate the outcome?

Skills

What skills must the learners master to demonstrate the intended outcome?

- Use conventions of grammar correctly
- Accept critical feedback
- Analyze across given criteria
- Write a short synopsis
- Write outline of plots
- Work in teams
- Design graphics
- Use marketing principles
- Create financial budgets

Assessment Tasks

What will learners do in here to demonstrate evidence of the outcome?

1. Deconstruct a script to evaluate and determine studio production value.
2. Produce a final marketing report for a film project, detailing a budget and steps for marketing the product.

Intended Outcomes

What do learners need to be able to DO "out there" in the rest of life that we're responsible for "in here"?

1. Analyze scripts worthy for production.
2. Edit scripts using correct grammar conventions.
3. Develop a marketing plan and budget for potential script productions.

POG/COG/WOG TITLE: COG: Aviation Maintenance Technology (AMT)   **Date:** _____

Concepts & Issues

What must the learners understand to demonstrate the intended outcome?

- Airframe systems
- Power plant systems
- Hydraulics
- Pneumatics
- Mechanics
- Fuel systems
- FAA constraints
- Inspections
- Repairs
- Safety
- 'Return to service' standard

- Safeguarding self and others
- Compliance with FAA and other related standards

What issues must the learners be able to resolve to demonstrate the outcome?

Skills

What skills must the learners master to demonstrate the intended outcome?

- Take mathematical measurements
- Operate tools safely
- Seek advice from others
- Access operating and FAA manuals to determine tolerances
- Document repairs in clear and concise writings
- Use electrical principles
- Apply hydraulic principles
- Apply mechanical principles with landing gear systems
- Use chemistry principles to address fuel systems issues

Assessment Tasks

What will learners do in here to demonstrate evidence of the outcome?

1. Submit appropriate documentation of procedures taken, consistent with legal, ethical, and FAA criteria in each lab.
2. Diagnose and troubleshoot three airframe and power plant systems with electrical, mechanical and hydraulic problems respectively.

Intended Outcomes

What do learners need to be able to DO "out there" in the rest of life that we're responsible for "in here"?

1. Apply electrical, mechanical, and hydraulic principles to the inspection, repair and troubleshooting of aircraft systems.
2. Make independent and accurate airframe and power plant airworthiness judgments.
3. Perform all skill operations to a 'return to service standard' using appropriate data, tools and equipment.
4. Perform inspections in accordance with legal, ethical and FAA constraints, data and standards.

POG/COG/WOG TITLE: COG: Composition (WR20–30) _____   **Date:** _____

Concepts & Issues

What must the learners understand to demonstrate the intended outcome?

- Grammaticality
- Main idea
- Supporting detail
- Organization
- Spelling (sound/spelling correspondences)
- Clarity in writing
- Variety in writing
- The need for writing in further education and the workplace

---

- Writer's block
- Fears of criticism
- Chaos in life
- Time
- Inability to organize
- Being overwhelmed
- Not understanding the college culture

What issues must the learners be able to resolve to demonstrate the outcome?

Skills

What skills must the learners master to demonstrate the intended outcome?

- Generate ideas for a paper
- Write clear main idea statements
- Provide support for ideas
- Organize support coherently
- Construct paragraphs and essays
- Identify and fix ungrammatical, punctuation, and spelling errors
- Think critically about one's own work
- Organize one's work

Assessment Tasks

What will learners do in here to demonstrate evidence of the outcome?

1. Write a clear paragraph out of class, with few grammatical errors.
2. Write a clear multi-paragraph essay out of class, with few grammatical errors.
3. Write a coherent essay on a given topic in an "on demand" situation.

Intended Outcomes

What do learners need to be able to DO "out there" in the rest of life that we're responsible for "in here"?

1. Communicate written thought in a clear and organized manner to effectively inform, persuade, describe, and convey ideas in academic, work, community, and family settings.
2. Gather, evaluate, and present own "body of work."
3. Take responsibility for own learning by: managing own time, managing materials, following directions, communicating effectively, persistently pursuing own goals.

POG/COG/WOG TITLE: COG: Yoga Teacher Training _____ **Date:** _____

Concepts & Issues

What must the learners understand to demonstrate the intended outcome?

- Definition of "yoga"
- Main objective of yoga
- Essential anatomy for yoga
- Joint and muscle safety
- Breathing –anatomy, physiology, techniques
- Prana & Pranayama
- Digestion and yoga
- Endocrine system and yoga
- Warm-up segment; Safety guidelines
- Standing poses; Seated poses Prone poses; Supine poses
- Sequencing; Sun salutations
- Meditation; Mantras Chakras; Guided relaxation
- Confident cuing

- Over-exertion
- Safety

What issues must the learners be able to resolve to demonstrate the outcome?

Skills

What skills must the learners master to demonstrate the intended outcome?

- Explain the importance of warm-up and stretch exercises
- Model basic yoga poses
- Adjust alignments of participants
- Correct participants' poses
- Explain and demonstrate the use of props in a class session
- Write yoga scripts
- Guided participants through meditation and closing activities
- Speak gently and calmly
- Select and use appropriate music

Assessment Tasks

What will learners do in here to demonstrate evidence of the outcome?

Design and guide students through

1) A set of warm-up activities (10 minutes)
2) A sequence of yoga poses (45 minutes)
3) Explain and make adjustments of poses in participants
4) A set of closing exercises (10 minutes)

Intended Outcomes

What do learners need to be able to DO "out there" in the rest of life that we're responsible for "in here"?

Design and teach safe and effective yoga classes for participants of all ages and abilities.

POG/COG/WOG TITLE: _____ **Date:** _____

COG: Computer Science (CS917) Micro-Computer Programming

Concepts & Issues

What must the learners understand to demonstrate the intended outcome?

- Computer architecture
- Assembly language
- Data transfers
- Integer mathematics
- Strings
- Conditioning
- Arrays
- Macros
- Micros
- Algorithms
- Viruses
- Processors
- Programming
- Flowcharting

- Resolve virus issues
- Interpret and resolve message errors

What issues must the learners be able to resolve to demonstrate the outcome?

Skills

What skills must the learners master to demonstrate the intended outcome?

- Use algorithms
- Apply algorithm design
- Flowchart a program
- Program INTEL-based computers
- Conduct online research
- Conduct debugging procedures
- Decipher machine code
- Assemble codes
- Test for viruses
- Load, copy, and move data

Assessment Tasks

What will learners do in here to demonstrate evidence of the outcome?

1. Troubleshoot the interaction between the assembly language and the operating system of a dysfunctional working computer.
2. Write a report on appropriate debugging procedures used.

Intended Outcomes

What do learners need to be able to DO "out there" in the rest of life that we're responsible for "in here"?

1. Design, develop, type, compile, and test assembly language programs.
2. Use online resources for studying microcomputer architecture and their respective assembly languages.

WOG: Performance Management: Coaching for Success

POG/COG/WOG TITLE: _____ **Date:** _____

Concepts & Issues

What must the learners understand to demonstrate the intended outcome?

- Performance
- Performance management
- Performance framework
- Expectations & Feedback
- Skills & Knowledge
- Tools & Resources
- Selection & Assignment
- Consequences & Incentives
- Motives & Preferences
- Performance issues
- Behaviors vs Skills
- Positive vs Constructive

- Timing of positive and constructive feedback
- Performance issues

What issues must the learners be able to resolve to demonstrate the outcome?

Skills

What skills must the learners master to demonstrate the intended outcome?

- Identify contributing factors that influence a performance issue
- Use positive reinforcement to reinforce good behaviors and skills
- Provide constructive feedback to improve behaviors and skills
- Establish behavioral incentives
- Model performance behaviors

Assessment Tasks

What will learners do in here to demonstrate evidence of the outcome?

1. Using the performance criteria of the scoring guide, determine the contributing factors for a given performance management issue.
2. Role-play1: Provide coaching assistance using positive and constructive feedback to improve a performance issue.
3. Role-play 2: Use positive reinforcement to recognize good work.

Intended Outcomes

What do learners need to be able to DO "out there" in the rest of life that we're responsible for "in here"?

1. Assess contributing factors to a performance issue.
2. Provide positive and constructive feedback using a coaching approach.

POG/COG/WOG TITLE: _____

WOG: Conscious Discipline: A Brain Smart Model

Date: _____

Concepts & Issues

What must the learners understand to demonstrate the intended outcome?

- Brain smart model
- Brain smart principles
- Connection
- Discipline
- Internal state
- Problem solving
- Empathy
- Survival state
- Emotional state
- Executive state

- Impulse control
- Safety
- Need for connection
- Power struggles
- Attachment
- Motivation

What issues must the learners be able to resolve to demonstrate the outcome?

Skills

What skills must the learners master to demonstrate the intended outcome?

- Become: Active calming
- See: A survival state responds to NOTICING
- Feel: An emotional state responds to EMPATHY
- Hear: An integrated executive state is able to PROBLEM SOLVE

Assessment Tasks

What will learners do in here to demonstrate evidence of the outcome?

Role-play and demonstrate the following four behaviors with a child:

1. Active calming by being a S.T.A.R. (Stop, Take a deep breath, And Relax).
2. Noticing with a partner.
3. Empathy by offering choices.
4. Reflect back what you hear the child saying by summarizing the essence of the child's statements.

Intended Outcomes

What do learners need to be able to DO "out there" in the rest of life that we're responsible for "in here"?

1. Examine, assess, and reflect on Brain States and their relevance to behavior.
2. Apply tools for managing the emotions of children.

POG/COG/WOG TITLE: WOG: Osteoporosis: Decreasing Its Risk _____ **Date:** _____

Concepts & Issues

What must the learners understand to demonstrate the intended outcome?

- Osteoporosis
- Bone loss
- Bone density
- Fracture(s)
- Diagnosis
- Prevention
- Treatment
- Calcium sources
- Hormones
- Estrogen
- Diet
- Exercise
- Symptoms

Risk factors
- Disregard for exercise and nutrition
- Lack of awareness about treatment

What issues must the learners be able to resolve to demonstrate the outcome?

Skills

What skills must the learners master to demonstrate the intended outcome?

- Self-assess using a questionnaire (Oregon Dairy Council)
- Interpret self-assessments to determine level of risk factors
- Conduct literature review on calcium sources
- Work in teams
- Critically analyze case studies.
- Analyze current statistical data on osteoporosis patterns in women and men
- Synthesize and summarize risk factors into treatment plans

Assessment Tasks

What will learners do in here to demonstrate evidence of the outcome?

Develop a 7-day health plan consistent with standardized health recommendations to reduce the risk of osteoporosis that includes:

1) Assessment of current osteoporosis patterns.
2) A set of routine exercise activities.
3) Intake of calcium (food/beverage) sources.

Intended Outcomes

What do learners need to be able to DO "out there" in the rest of life that we're responsible for "in here"?

1. Calculate and compare one's daily calcium intake to current recommended health standards.
2. Incorporate daily actions one can personally take to decrease the risk of osteoporosis.
3. Manage a routine plan for consuming calcium sources to reduce the risk of osteoporosis.

POG/COG/WOG TITLE: WOG: Aging Traffic Offenders

Date: _____

Concepts & Issues

What must the learners understand to demonstrate the intended outcome?

- Aging changes
- Technology changes
- Violation consequences
- Values, beliefs, attitudes and behaviors
- Most common violations that bring injury

- Medications
- Flexibility/strength
- Vision/hearing
- Confidence
- Roadway design
- Vehicle technologies
- Distractions

What issues must the learners be able to resolve to demonstrate the outcome?

Skills

What skills must the learners master to demonstrate the intended outcome?

- Complete a vehicle safety check.
- Demonstrate strategies to reduce visual impairments.
- Research and plan for other modes of transportation.

Assessment Tasks

What will learners do in here to demonstrate evidence of the outcome?

1. Complete a self-assessment tool that identifies your own age related issues.
2. Identify the personal actions you will take to increase driving safety and avoid further violation of traffic ordinances.

Intended Outcomes

What do learners need to be able to DO "out there" in the rest of life that we're responsible for "in here"?

1. Keep yourself and others safe by driving in compliance with all traffic rules and regulations.
2. Continuously assess your physical and mental age-related changes as they affect your ability to drive safely.

The CONTENT Primer: Aligning Essential Content with Learning Outcomes

Our Preferred Terms for Determining Essential Content

Term	Meaning
Academic program	A highly organized set of learning experiences learners navigate through that usually culminates in a specific degree or certificate.
Accountability	The institutional responsibility to stakeholders for the results it produces. The institution defines its intended outcomes and provides appropriate information about results to key stakeholders.
Assessment	Ongoing process aimed at understanding and improving student learning for systematically gathering, analyzing and interpreting evidence of intended learning outcomes.
Assessment tasks	Complex and significant tasks learners complete to demonstrate the intended outcome (e.g. projects, portfolios, presentations, problem solutions, demonstrations, simulations, role-plays). Often referred to as performance tasks.
Backward design	A process of beginning with an intended outcome, then working backward to determine appropriate assessment tasks and essential content (concepts to be learned, issues to be solved and skills to be mastered); a process used at the organization, program and course level.
Competencies	A term mistakenly used as a synonym for outcomes. They consist largely of miniscule tasks the learner is asked to demonstrate for a grade.
Competency-based framework	A curriculum design approach that consists of demonstrating a set of specific isolated tasks for mastery of content to be learned.
Concepts	Ideas that learners must understand in order to achieve the intended outcome; emphasis on depth of understanding rather than breadth of information.
Conceptual learning	A learning strategy as well as a form of critical thinking in which individuals learn how to categorize and organize information in logical mental structures.

Our Preferred Terms for Determining Essential Content

Term	Meaning
Conceptual thinking	A specific type of thought that involves reflection, abstraction, critical thinking, and problem solving.
Critical thinking	A form of thinking that involves analysis, synthesis, evaluation and reflection.
Content-based framework	A curriculum design approach which consists largely of topics to be covered, readings on the topics, term papers on the topics and objective tests about the topics.
Course Outcome Guide (COG)	A tool for collaboratively developing a one-page plan focusing on intended learning outcomes and working backwards to determine essential course content.
Guide's *guide*	A term used to describe the essential role that learning outcomes play in guiding learners.
Issues	Problems and challenges that learners must be able to resolve in order to achieve the intended outcome.
Knowledge base	Facts and information learners need to know to understand the major concepts and issues, and develop the skill sets.
Lean learning	An approach to curriculum design in which less content is better than more in the promotion of deep understanding.
Learner's journey	A flow of learning events that learners navigate through to achieve the intended learning outcomes.
Learning outcomes	Statements that describe a vision of what learners will be able to do outside the classroom (in real-life roles) as the result of their learning. Learning outcomes are short, concise and detailed descriptions that provide the road map for guiding course, program, and institutional level learning.

Our Preferred Terms for Determining Essential Content

Term	Meaning
Lifelong learner	A person who is motivated to pursue learning voluntarily, for both personal and professional reasons, throughout life.
Outcome-based framework	A curriculum design approach which begins with a vision of what we hope the learner will be able to DO outside and beyond the classroom, in real-life roles, with what s/he learns in a program, course, or workshop/training.
Outside-in design	Curriculum design process that begins by envisioning what the learners need to be able to do "out there" (outside the classroom) in the rest of life.
Program Outcome Guide (POG)	A one-page plan focusing on the intended program learning outcomes and working backward to determine essential content for a program.
Real-life roles	The roles that our learners take on in their personal and/or work lives, such as *family member, life-long learner, supervisor, medical assistant, etc.*
Scoring guide	A qualitative assessment tool that explicitly describes the standards for good performance to help the learner know what "good" looks like; can be used by learners, evaluators, or assessors to provide feedback to improve performance or product.
Session Outcome Guide (SOG)	A tool for developing a one-page plan focusing on intended learning outcomes and working backwards to determine essential content for a class session.
Skills	Abilities that are essential to the outcome, usually learned and mastered through practice and feedback. Combined with what the learner must understand (concepts and issues), these form the content of the learning experience.
Stakeholders/Constituents	Parts of the larger system that have an invested interest in the outcomes of a specific educational and/or workplace training program: community, families, students, employers, professions/trades, taxpayers, society, global community.
Workshop Outcome Guide (WOG)	A tool for developing a one-page plan focusing on intended learning outcomes and working backwards to determine essential content for a workshop or training.

We attempt in this section to acknowledge the works of a number of authors who have influenced our thinking on outcome-based curriculum design, stretching across a broad educational spectrum from learning theory and conceptual thinking to new and emerging paradigm shifts. Most importantly, it has confirmed our belief that analyzing learning outcomes to determine the essential content in curriculum design is paramount for effective learning to occur. These works have helped us think more systemically about what teaching and learning should mean in the 21st century.

Influences of Constructivist Learning Theory on Curriculum Design

Ausubel, David P. (1968). *Educational psychology: a cognitive view*. Chicago, IL: Holt, Rinehart, and Winston.

Brandon, Amy F. & All, Anita C. (2010). Constructivism theory analysis and application to curricula. Nursing Education Perspectives, 31 (2), 89–92.

Getha-Eby, Teresa J.; Beery, Theresa; Xu, Yin; & O'Brien, Beth A. (2014). Meaningful learning: theoretical support for concept-based teaching. Journal of Nursing Education, 53 (9), 494–500.

Hardin, Pamela K. & Richardson, Stephanie J. (2012). Teaching the concept curricula: Theory and method. Journal of Nursing Education, 51 (3), 155–59.

Marlowe, Bruce A. & Page, Marilyn L. (2005). *Creating and Sustaining the Constructivist Classroom*, (2nd ed.). Corwin Press, A Sage Publications Company: Thousand Oaks, California.

Tobias, Sigmund & Duffy, Thomas M. (2009). *Constructivist Instruction, Success or Failure?* Routledge, Taylor & Francis Group: New York and London.

Willis, Jerry W. (2009). *Constructivist Instructional Design (C-ID)*. Information Age Publishing: Charlotte, North Carolina.

Influences of Conceptual Thinking on Curriculum Design

Bristol, Tim J. & Rosati, L. Jane, (2013). Successful concept-based learning through the integration of technology. Teaching and Learning in Nursing, 8 (3), 112–16.

Costa, Arthur L. & Liebmann, Rosemarie M. (1997). *Envisioning Process as Content*. Corwin Press, A Sage Publications Company: Thousand Oaks, California.

Dailey, Janine L. The concept-based curriculum: key points for a transition. Retrieved from: *http://academicconsulting.elsevier.com*

Diekelmann, Nancy. (2002). Too much content…. Epistemologies' grasp and nursing education. Journal of Nursing Education, 41 (11), 469–70.

Erickson, H. Lynn. (2007). *Concept-based curriculum and instruction for the thinking classroom*. Corwin Press: Thousand Oaks, CA.

Getha-Eby, Teresa J.; Beery, Theresa; Xu, Yin; & O'Brien, Beth A. (2014). Meaningful learning: theoretical support for concept-based teaching. Journal of Nursing Education, 53 (9), 494–500.

Giddens, Jean F.; Caputi, Linda; & Rodgers, Beth. (2015) Mastering concept-based teaching. St. Louis, MO, Elsevier/Mosby. Nursing Education Perspectives, 31(6), 372–77.

Giddens, Jean F. & Brady, Debra. P. (2007). Rescuing nursing education from content saturation: the case for a concept-based curriculum. Journal of Nursing Education, 46 (2), 65–69.

Giddens, Jean F.; Wright, Mary; & Gray, Irene. (2012). Selecting concepts for a concept-based curriculum: application of a benchmark approach. Journal of Nursing Education, 51 (9), 511–15.

Hardin, Pamela K. & Richardson, Stephanie J. (2012). Teaching the concept curricula: Theory and method. Journal of Nursing Education, 51 (3), 155–59.

Ironside, Pamela M. (2004). Covering content and teaching thinking: deconstructing the additive curriculum. Journal of Nursing Education, 43 (1), 5–12.

Nelson, Regina K., Chesler, Naomi C., & Strang, Kevin T. (2013). Development of concept-based physiology lessons for biomedical engineering undergraduate students. Advanced Physiology Education, 37 (2), 176–83.

Influences in New and Emerging Curriculum Design

Brady, Debra; Welborn-Brown, Pauline; Smith, Debra; Giddens, Jean; Harris, Judith; Wright, Mary; & Nichols, Ruth. (2008). Staying afloat: surviving curriculum change. Nurse Educator, 33(5), 198–201.

Erickson, H. Lynn. (2008). *Stirring the Head, Heart, and Soul*. Corwin Press: Thousand Oaks, California.

Freeman, Linda H.; Voignier, Ruth R.; & Scott,Deborah L. (2002). New curriculum for a new century: beyond repackaging. Journal of Nursing Education, 41(1), 38–40.

Schmidt, William H., McKnight, Curtis C. & Raizen, Senta. (1997). *A splintered vision: an investigation of U.S. science and mathematics education*. U.S. National Research Center for the Third International Mathematics and Science Study (TIMSS). Dordrecht, Netherlands, Kluwer Academic Publishers.

Sportsman, Susan. Concept-based curricula in Nursing: perceptions of the trend. Retrieved from: *http://academicconsulting.elsevier.com*.

Stanley, Mary Jo C. & Dougherty, Jacalyn P. (2010). A paradigm shift in nursing education: a new model. Nursing Education Perspective, 31 (6), 378–80.

Stokowski, Laura A. (2011). Overhauling nursing education. Nurse Educator, 36 (3), 111.

Acknowledgments

Our thanks go to the hundreds of individuals in colleges, agencies and industry who, through our teaching and consulting experiences with them, have helped to shape our understanding of learning outcomes and assessment over the years. Without these experiences, we would have had nothing at all to say.

As just one part of a six-part series, this Primer wasn't created by us alone. We are deeply indebted to our full team on the *OUTCOME Primer Series 2.0*: Lori Sours, Don Prickel, Kathy Telban, Lynn Null, Geoffrey Floyd and Robin McBride. This team has never failed to inspire us. They have each demonstrated a high level of intellectual honesty concerning our work and have paddled the rapids with us on the way to the take-out.

Additional credit goes to members of the faculty and staff at Central Oregon Community College in providing opportunities for us to implement many of the concepts and ideas expressed in this work. A special thanks to: Laura Boehme, Michael Fisher, Jennifer Newby, Tony Russell, Alisa Schneider, and Vickery Viles for sharing in this quest!

—Michele Decker,
Ruth Stiehl
2017

Ruth E. Stiehl, Ed.D.

PROFESSOR EMERITUS, INSTRUCTIONAL SYSTEMS, OREGON STATE UNIVERSITY

CO-FOUNDER, WHITE WATER INSTITUTE FOR LEADERSHIP TRAINING
FOUNDER, THE LEARNING ORGANIZATION

Dr. Stiehl, a thought leader on learning outcomes assessment for over twenty years, was lead author on the acclaimed original series of THE OUTCOME PRIMERS. Over a period of fifteen years this original series guided colleges across the United States and Canada as they prepared for new accreditation standards for outcomes assessment. Along with a team of new co-authors and consultants at The Learning Organization, she has expanded the work beyond colleges to workplace training, including agencies, business and industry. In contrast to the work of many academics, all of the writing, speaking and workshops produced by The Learning Organization are charged with story, metaphor, and integrated learning. Dr. Stiehl lives and works in Corvallis, Oregon.

Michele Decker, RN, MSN, MEd

OUTCOME STRATEGIST, THE LEARNING ORGANIZATION

PROFESSOR OF NURSING, CENTRAL OREGON COMMUNITY COLLEGE

Michele Decker is a Professor of Nursing at Central Oregon Community College where she teaches in an Associate of Applied Science in Nursing program. She serves as a faculty leader in outcome-based curriculum development across her campus. Reaching out to colleagues and supporting them in their curriculum work is very important to Michele. She believes that faculty level leadership, and a faculty level perspective, is key to sustaining outcomes and assessment practices across all colleges.

Nation-wide, nurse educators have been the early adopters of outcome-based, concept-focused learning and quality assessment, and are providing support to other disciplines. It's Michele's intent to continue this leadership through consulting and writing. Michele lives and works in Bend, Oregon.

Authors can be contacted at *strategists@outcomeprimers.com*.

Don Prickel, Ph.D.
EXECUTIVE EDITOR

Dr. Prickel, one of the lead authors in the Outcome Primers Series 2.0, has also served in the major role of executive editor for all six primers, assuring continuity within the series. He brings to this work many years of experience as an adult educator and consultant to colleges and universities on instructional strategies and adult learning theory.

The authors of *The OUTCOME Primers Series 2.0* are available to consult in person with you and your organization in the following ways:

- Facilitating work sessions in outcomes and assessment planning at any level of the organization
- Face-to-face and on-line coaching, advising, and providing counsel to leaders, committees, and instructors on outcomes and assessment

Contact us through our website:
www.outcomeprimers.com
or
email us at: *strategists@outcomeprimers.com*

Made in the USA
San Bernardino, CA
26 August 2018